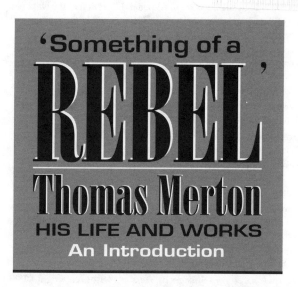

'Something of a

REBEL'

Thomas Merton

HIS LIFE AND WORKS

An Introduction

William H. Shannon

ST. ANTHONY MESSENGER PRESS

Cincinnati, Ohio

What Critics Say About *'Something of a Rebel'*

"As the editor and publisher of Thomas Merton's first (and still most popular) book, *The Seven Storey Mountain*, I find William Shannon's new book, *'Something of a Rebel,'* a lively, informative and enlightening introduction to the life and writings of the most widely read spiritual writer of this century. As the general editor of Thomas Merton's letters, William Shannon is recognized as a leading authority on Merton's life and works. His understanding of Merton's complex character is superb."

—*Robert Giroux, Farrar, Straus & Giroux, Inc.*

"This is a superb introduction to perhaps the greatest and most influential spiritual writer of the passing century. Merton, truly human in his strengths and in his weaknesses, will continue to speak no less powerfully through the next. He was a rebel, but a trustworthy rebel, because he was a contemplative who could discern the hidden ground of God's love even in the disconnected individualism and apocalyptic violence of his times and ours. I know of no one who can introduce us more adequately to Merton, and with greater wisdom, wit and freshness of outlook, than William Shannon."

—*Ross Mackenzie, director of the department of religion, Chautauqua Institution*

"William Shannon has performed a wonderful service to potential readers who are drawn to the Thomas Merton story, yet may feel snowed in by the hundreds of books written by and about the extraordinary writer/monk. Where to begin? I'd suggest starting with Shannon's *'Something of a Rebel.'* With a winning combination of affection for his subject and an appreciation of its complexities, Shannon succeeds in his dual purposes of introducing us to Merton's life and writing and appraising the relevance of Merton's message to our own human struggles and spiritual journeys. In an engaging personal voice, Shannon serves as a guide through Merton's amazing biography, the gallery of major themes that occupied Merton as a writer, and the library of his major books—all of which combine to make Thomas Merton a centrifugal force in American letters whose influence continues to reach wider and wider audiences of women and men who, like Merton and Shannon, struggle for moral and spiritual meaning during troubled, turbulent and confused times."

—*David D. Cooper, professor and acting director, The American Studies Program, Michigan State University*

Contents

Foreword

In my estimation, of all the terms one could use to describe William H. Shannon—priest, professor, author, retreat master, chaplain—the one that most fittingly describes him is: disciple of Jesus. This diocesan priest of Rochester, New York, has spent his entire adult life ministering to students at Nazareth College and, after his retirement from the classroom, he continues to act as chaplain to the Sisters of St. Joseph, whose motherhouse is on the Nazareth campus, while lecturing, writing and giving retreats.

Anyone fortunate enough to spend a few hours in his study cluttered with books, icons, CDs and Merton memorabilia (his books spill over to the dining room across the hall!) would be in the company of a deeply learned, holy (I do not use that term easily!), peace-filled person. He is one who in his life combines a deep spirit of prayer, a passion for peace, an openness to all whom he meets, and a keen Irish wit.

In the late Trappist monk Thomas Merton, Bill Shannon has found a kindred spirit. Few know more about Merton's life and writings and fewer still have grasped how important Merton is as a resource for understanding what it means to be a Christian disciple. Shannon's deep encounter with Merton's work over the years has resulted in many significant publications. Not only has he published a collection of Merton's writings on peace and social activism, but he has served as general editor of Merton's letters. He has also written *Thomas Merton's Dark Path* and the useful biography of Merton, *Silent Lamp*.

The readers it is hoped this book will reach are older and

younger persons who up to now have never had contact with Merton. It is also for those who may have read a bit of Merton—perhaps many years ago—but failed to follow up on that initial contact.

Still another readership the author would like to reach out to is the generation of younger readers who have never been introduced to Thomas Merton. Merton loved young people and from his monastery reached out to them. While in the monastery he found great delight in working with the young novices who came under his care. Merton's desire to love God and others, to be alert to suffering and injustice, to learn and listen, to strive for compassion, to be a lover of poetry and people, to watch the world of nature, to be deeply committed—these are all qualities that inspire young and old alike.

Readers of Shannon's 'Something of a Rebel' will see these ideals in Merton and, if they are fortunate, they will be inspired to live these ideals in their own lives. After all, how could one not love a monk who, writing to a friend about some young men at the monastery, describes them as having an intense interest "in wildlife and professional football and no obvious signs whatever of piety," and pronounces them "good prospects"?

Lawrence S. Cunningham
Chair and Professor of Theology
University of Notre Dame
December 4, 1996

Introduction

"He was something of a legendary figure among the old boys[1] of his generation and he was clearly something of a rebel." These words, written on March 3, 1942, by G. Talbot Griffith, headmaster of Oakham School in the Midlands of England, were part of a letter sent to the Catholic Bishop of Nottingham in England to be forwarded to the abbot at the Abbey of Our Lady of Gethsemani. It was one of several letters of reference required by canon law before the twenty-five-year-old Thomas Merton could be accepted as a novice into the Gethsemani community. Ten years earlier Thomas Merton had completed his studies at Oakham. Ten years is a short time in which to become "a legendary figure." It may well be that the reason he became a legendary figure was the reputation he acquired as "something of a rebel."

Writing this book some fifty-four years after Mr. Griffith sent his letter, I would venture the opinion that time has proved that Oakham's headmaster, without realizing it, I am sure, was uttering prophetic words that continue to be true. In the more than half-century since Griffith wrote, Merton has indeed become a "legendary figure" with numerous stories—many true, some highly questionable—continuing to accumulate around this unusual monk. Moreover, the reputation he had acquired at Oakham as a "rebel" did not cease to be true when he became a monk. He may have doffed the rebel's cap when he first entered the monastery, but not for long. Through much of his monastic life, and especially in his later years, he continued to be "something of a rebel." Joan Baez, the American folk singer and social activist, visited Merton in 1967. Reflecting on that visit, she remarked: "He was a rebel. And I imagine [this] man tucked so far away [in a monastery] gave priests and nuns and other church people the courage to take steps they wouldn't otherwise have taken" (*Merton: By Those Who Knew Him Best*, ed. Paul Wilkes [San Francisco: Harper and Row, 1984], p. 43).

I am letting the words of the headmaster of Oakham, abetted by Joan Baez's remarks, influence my choice of the title for this book, whose intent is to introduce the reader to Thomas Merton and to suggest ways in which his life story and his writings can help us on our spiritual journey.

Some might question my using the word "rebel" in the title of a book about Gethsemani's famous monk. After all, in terms of its etymology, the word takes on a rather harsh, perhaps even sinister, meaning. It derives from the Latin *rebellare* which means "to make war." It can mean "to resist, even to defy, authority." Describing Merton as a "rebel" in such terms might turn some people off and away from this book. This is something I certainly don't want to do!

But the word "rebel" can also take on a milder, but still strong, meaning: "resisting accepted conventions." In this sense the word "rebel" can be used to describe people who ask questions about established ways of doing things. They may do this because they have an insight into reality not shared by those who are content to do things "the way we have always done them." They may see, for instance, that certain accepted ways of doing things have lost their original meaning and need to be rethought. They refuse to be stuck in past practices that have lost the power to meet the needs of a very different present. Rebels can change the course of history, sometimes for good, sometimes for ill. Rebels are often prophets. But, of course, there are true prophets and false prophets. It is only time that eventually distinguishes the one from the other.

In what ways was Merton a "rebel"? Most especially in his refusal in any aspect of his life to be bound by a past that was static and lifeless. This does not mean that he lacked a strong sense of tradition. On the contrary, tradition was very important to him, but tradition as something living and vibrant. He refused to be content with the *status quo* when it no longer nourished the human spirit. Merton did not rebel against Christian faith, yet he refused to accept it unreflectively, for he knew that it would influence his life only to the degree that he made it truly his own. Merton did not rebel against authority, yet he questioned a blind, unthinking obedience, whether in the monastery or in state or Church. He did not rebel against the monastic life; yet in his later years he saw the need of major reforms if monasticism was to survive as a viable force in contemporary human society. Jean Leclercq has said: "Merton was a free man. A very good Trappist, he joined with joy and swallowed everything—at the beginning. After a few years he started asking: 'Why that, Why this?' Not to destroy, not even to criticize, but just to try to justify" (Ibid., p. 130). And what he could not justify, he looked to change. He was not afraid to enter into uncharted waters, when he believed that this was the way to go. And this is part of the excitement generated by the man with whom we shall be living through this book.

Most rebels are difficult people to live with: Often they are so intense about the cause they espouse that they are unable to relax or let others do so in their company. There was surely this intensity in Thomas Merton concerning issues to which he felt strong and enthusiastic commitments. Yet I dare say that his saving grace was his wonderful sense of humor (something lacking in all too many rebels). He was able to laugh at himself: He did his best not to take himself too seriously. If he was a rebel, he was always (well, almost always) a "gracious" rebel. He did his best to persuade, and often (though not always), his persuasive powers were strong. Yet he never sought to impose his views. He lent an open ear to those who might disagree with him. There was a sense of goodwill and brightness of character that made him a happy person and a genial sort of rebel. "He was," says Dom John Eudes Bamberger, "an outgoing person with an obvious ease with relationships, very approachable, with a great sense of humor" (Ibid., p. 116).

It is my hope that that approachability, that sense of humor, coupled with a strong sense of purpose and commitment, may light up these pages as we make friends with one of the great spiritual writers, not only of the present century, but also, I dare say, of the century that will soon be upon us.

Just a brief word about the intent of this book. I was asked to write a book that would introduce Thomas Merton to people who knew him but slightly or perhaps not at all. My purpose, then, is to present Merton's life story (Chapter One) to suggest that this mid-twentieth-century writer can speak meaningfully to women and men on the verge of a new century (Chapter Two), to develop in my own way some of the themes that make their way through his writings (Chapter Three), and to suggest what books one ought to read first as one enters into the huge library of Mertoniana (Chapter Four).[2]

The readers I hope to reach are intelligent and inquiring women and men who want to be challenged by one of the great thinkers and spiritual writers of the twentieth century. I shall do my best to make Merton's life and works come alive for you, dear reader. If this fails to happen, the fault will be mine, not Merton's.

Notes

[1] That is, the alumni.

[2] At a time when inclusive language is accepted as a norm, it is a bit disconcerting to note the lack of such usage in much of Merton's writing. In fairness to him, we must acknowledge that he lived in an age that had not yet discovered the importance of inclusive language. I believe it is only right to leave his writings as he wrote them. I hope that those who find occasional texts bothersome will understand why I have chosen to leave the text untouched and will feel free, in reading the Merton text, to make for themselves whatever adjustments will make them more comfortable.

CHAPTER ONE

The Life Story

The Merton story divides itself into two almost equal parts: (1) the years before he entered the monastery—from January 31, 1915, to December 9, 1941 (just a month and a few days short of his twenty-seventh birthday); and (2) the years in the monastery—from December 10, 1941, to December 10, 1968 (exactly twenty-seven years).

1. The Pre-Monastic Years

Where do you begin telling the story of a person's life? The logical point is at the beginning—with that person's birth. For Merton the birth date is January 31, 1915; the place of birth, Prades in the south of France. But in telling the Merton story, I have decided against starting at the beginning. Instead, I would like to bring readers into that story at a significant point almost midway into his life. This will offer something of a center from which we can move backward to see what brought him to this point and forward to know where it would lead him.

A Cottage in Olean, New York, 1939

I invite you to the town of Olean in southwest New York State, more specifically, to the picturesque hills above the city and toward the south. An area of rare beauty. The rolling hills, reaching all the way to the Pennsylvania border, are covered with miles of forest, evergreens and oak trees, and full of oil. Living in these hills one hears, night and day, the rhythm of the oil wells, "the heart-beat of the hills."

Two or three miles into the hills outside of Olean, west of the road and set off in the trees, is a large red cottage that belonged to Benjie Marcus. Marcus was brother-in-law to Robert Lax and most generous in loaning out the cottage to Lax and his friends.

That is how it happened that in 1939, Bob Lax, Ed Rice and Tom Merton (twenty-two years of age at the time) spent most of the summer at the cottage. They had been fellow students at Columbia University and were close friends. There was plenty of room: The cottage was big and had a large porch. Eating, drinking, reading, writing, discussing art, literature, poetry and the war in Europe, playing jazz records, staying up until all hours—that was their daily horarium. There were regular visits into Olean to collect mail, to get provisions (including plenty of beer and a bit of scotch) and, not infrequently, to see a movie. Olean was a sleepy, laid-back town, offering few attractions to these sophisticated New Yorkers. Hence, much of their time was spent pounding their typewriters to see who would be the one to write the great novel of the century. Lax's novel was called *The Spangled Palace* and was about a traveling nightclub. Rice was working on *The Blue Horse*, the story of a race around the world. Merton, after discarding two earlier titles, announced to his fellow-authors that his novel would be called *The Labyrinth*.

~~~~~~ Looking Back: The Ways of Grace ~~~~~~

It had been a happy Merton who had come to Olean that summer. The previous year, 1938, had been, in many ways, the most memorable of his life. In January 1938 he had graduated from Columbia with his B.A. degree and immediately had enrolled in the Graduate School and had begun work on his M.A. degree, for which he had written a dissertation on William Blake. It had been completed that year and in February 1939 he had received his graduate degree. Also, 1938 had been the year in which Merton met Bramachari, the Hindu monk (just arrived in America from

India), who encouraged Merton to read the Christian mystical writings before trying to make sense out of the texts of eastern religions—advice that proved most beneficial. But most memorable of all had been the event of November 16, 1938: his reception into the Roman Catholic Church by Father Joseph P. Moore at Corpus Christi Church on West 121st Street in New York City.

People who had known Merton just six years earlier (in 1933) when he was at Clare College, Cambridge, would have been stunned to hear that he had taken this step. His Cambridge days scarcely gave even the slightest inklings that such a future was in store for him. His British friends would have remembered him as one who frequented too many pubs and was the life of too many wild parties that lasted well into the night.

Chapter Four of his novel *The Labyrinth* (which was largely autobiographical and which was to remain unpublished) is entitled "The Party in the Night." Pages appear to be missing at the beginning of the chapter. But Naomi Burton Stone, Merton's literary agent who read the manuscript in its entirety, vividly remembers the account of a wild party, where a mock crucifixion took place. Was Merton the one who was crucified? No one knows. There is the interesting fact that when Merton made application for permanent residence in the United States, the Declaration of Intention he had to sign had a space for identifying "visible distinctive marks." The distinctive mark mentioned on Merton's Declaration was "a scar on the palm of the right hand." A similar description appears on his naturalization papers of June 26, 1951, the day he became an American citizen. This is highly circumstantial and I would not want to offer it as definitive evidence that Merton was the principal actor in this bizarre event. But the kind of life Merton was living at the time might well suggest him as a possible candidate for this gruesome role.

One thing we can be certain of: Tom Merton's life up to his early twenties had been a life without discipline. With no clear goals in life, he had followed his own whims and fancies. He was adrift, rudderless and without direction, on a sea of aimlessness and amorality and with no religious faith at all. Many people—teachers, fellow-students, friends—must have wondered what would happen to this young man, so bright and talented, and yet so unruly and intractable.

Then, like a bolt out of the blue, they had heard that he had been received into the Catholic Church. They must surely have wondered: Is this the Merton we knew? What happened to him? What in the world possessed him to take this step? Questions of this sort evoke no simple answer, no adequate explanation. Can anyone unwrap the mystery of a deep spiritual conversion that takes place—seemingly all of a sudden—in a person's life? Can the person himself or herself even explain it? Perhaps all that can be said about Merton's conversion is that there were many factors at work that gradually and steadily had led him to this decisive moment.

The Grace of Books

Books had always been, and always would remain, a strong influence in Merton's life. His reading had played a significant role in his journey to conversion. It may have been his reading of Etienne Gilson's *The Spirit of Medieval Philosophy* that started him on his way. For it gave him what no one had given him before: an insight into the meaning of God. It convinced him that belief in God was intellectually respectable. If Gilson helped to clear his head, Aldous Huxley's *Ways and Means* may be said to have opened his heart to the possibility of a higher way of life lived at a deeper level of consciousness. Merton delighted in the goal Huxley set before him. Still, he was not quite ready for the way Huxley suggested as the only means of achieving this goal, namely, a life of discipline. As Augustine had prayed at one point in his life: "Lord, make me chaste, but not yet," so Merton might have prayed for discipline in his life, but not yet. But that would come and sooner than anyone, including himself, might have expected.

The Grace of Teachers and Influential Friends

Perhaps more important than his readings had been the personal influences that had come into his life after he had left England and had become, in January 1934, a student at Columbia University. How fortunate young people are who cross paths with teachers who challenge them and energize them and enable them to discover gifts and talents they never realized they had. Good teachers change lives. I have had many classroom teachers in my life. I am grateful to all of them. But there is one I hold in special memory and esteem. The great gift he gave to me was a love of good literature and a desire to write. Just one special teacher: For some people that is enough. It was, I believe, for me.

Of special importance in Merton's life were two teachers at Columbia: Mark Van Doren, the distinguished professor of English literature, and Daniel Walsh, a part-time teacher of philosophy. Their classes and his conversations with them had opened his eyes to the shallowness of the life he had been living. Contact with them strengthened his growing resolve to bring into his life what he had been shrinking from: the discipline he had read about in Huxley's book. Merton's friendship with these two men lasted throughout the rest of his life. He kept in touch with them even after he entered the monastery.

There were other human factors, too, that subtly, perhaps unconsciously, had moved him in the direction of Catholic faith. One of these, most assuredly, was the commitment of a few small groups of Catholics to involvement in the social concerns of the day, especially the care of the poor. There were the people at Friendship House in Harlem, founded by the Baroness de Hueck, and there were the Catholic Worker people in the Lower East Side of New York City, under the leadership of that valiant and inspiring woman who exercised a truly prophetic role in the American Church for half a century, Dorothy Day. Almost thirty years after his reception into the Church, Merton wrote to Dorothy Day: "If there were no *Catholic Worker* and such forms of witness, I would never have joined the Catholic Church" (Letter of

December 29, 1965, *The Hidden Ground of Love*, p. 151).

Conversion as Grace

> God called out to me from His own immense depths.
> (*The Seven Storey Mountain*)

Of course the all-important factor in Merton's acceptance of
Catholic faith had been the grace of God, though we must not
forget that grace operates, not in a vacuum, but in the
concrete details of a person's life and relationships. At any
rate, at long last, on the sixteenth day of November in 1938,
Merton had yielded to the grace that, he had come to realize,
had been pursuing him for a long time. The story of that day
of his reception into the Catholic Church he narrates in
moving, passionate prose in his autobiography, *The Seven
Storey Mountain*. He closes with a momentous summing up of
the day: "And God called out to me from His own immense
depths" (p. 225). This statement is significant not only as a
summary of the baptismal day. It could well serve as a
description of the rest of his life—God calling out to him
from the immense depths of divinity. It is a statement that
embodies his message, too: It goes to the heart of his writings.
In 1963 Merton said:

> Whatever I may have written, I think all can be reduced in
> the end to this one root truth: that God calls human
> persons to union with Himself and with one another in
> Christ....

On May 25, 1939, Tom Merton had been confirmed by Bishop
Stephen J. Donahue at Corpus Christi Church. Having been
baptized Thomas, he chose James as his confirmation name.
For a while after, he signed his name Thomas James Merton,
instead of T. F. Merton.

~~~~~~~~ The Cottage in Olean ~~~~~~~~

It had been the still-lingering glow of that great grace that
Merton had brought with him to the cottage "writers' studio"

in the summer of 1939. Tom had already written several novels, none of which had found a publisher. Neither would the one he worked on in that summer of 1939, *The Labyrinth*. As far as I know, none of these novels exists in its entirety, but reading what remains of them, one soon gets the point that they are all pretty much the same novel: They tell his own life story. It is quite appropriate, therefore, for us—as we think of him at the cottage in Olean in 1939—to go back and bring his story up to date.

~~~~~~~~~~~ ***Looking Back Again*** ~~~~~~~~~~~~

Surely, as he wrote he recalled Prades in France, the place of his birth on the last day of January 1915. He knew, too, how, when he was but a year and a half old, his parents braved the submarine-infested waters of the Atlantic to bring him to the United States to live: for a time with his maternal grandparents and then for a few short years in their own home in Flushing, New York.

A word about his parents: Ruth Jenkins, Tom's mother, had left her Douglaston, Long Island, home to go to France to study art. At an art studio presided over by Percyval Tudor-Hart, she met the man whom she would marry and whose sons she would bear. Owen Merton was a British Commonwealth citizen, born in New Zealand and carrying a British passport. Like Ruth he had come to Paris because he wanted to be an artist. Having followed Tudor-Hart to London where he had moved his studio, they were married at St. Anne's Church in Soho, the west-central district of London, on April 7, 1914. After their marriage, they returned to France and settled in Prades where, on the last day of January 1915, their first son was born. Ruth insisted that he be named Tom, not Thomas. It is so recorded in the birth registry at Prades. His godfather, later to be his guardian, was Tom Izod Bennett, a London physician who had been a classmate of Owen in New Zealand.

The Death of Ruth Merton

Home in America, Ruth gave birth to a second son, John Paul, on November 2, 1918. Two years later, when she and Owen were contemplating a return to France, Ruth became terminally ill with stomach cancer. She succumbed to the disease on October 3, 1921. Her death left Tom with a weight of sadness and perplexity. Ruth, despite the sometimes stern demands she made on her son, was the source of stability in the family. Now she was gone and Tom was only six years of age.

I cannot help but wonder if the lives of Tom and John Paul would not have been very different if their mother had not contracted cancer and had lived a normal lifespan. She was a strong woman (Tom thought of her as "severe"); she would have kept the family together and given them a normal family environment. With her death that ceased to be a possibility. Owen, while he sincerely desired to be a good father and gave it an honest try, desperately wanted, at the same time, to be a distinguished artist. That he had the talent to achieve this goal is abundantly clear from the many watercolors of his that are available, though unfortunately scattered among many owners.

Owen Merton: A Man of Conflicts

Good father, distinguished artist—two noble ambitions, but unfortunately not easily harmonized. More often than not the artistic desire won out over the familial one. In June 1930 an entire issue of the quarterly magazine *Art in New Zealand* was devoted to Owen's art. There were ample illustrations of Owen's work and an extensive article about him by James Shelley (a writer for the quarterly, not otherwise identified). Shelley's concluding words captured the intensity of Owen's devotion to art.

> To a man like Merton, art is no soft mistress to be trifled with, but a tyrannizing goddess who exacts the last ounce of energy in worshiping devotion.

Yielding all too readily to the blandishments of this "tyrannizing goddess," Owen was often an absentee father, with the children left to the care of others: their maternal grandparents, Sam ("Pop") and Martha ("Bonnemaman") Jenkins, or boarding schools. Many years later (in 1966), now living as a hermit at Gethsemani, Merton wrote: "I realized today after Mass what a desperate, despairing childhood I had around the ages of seven—nine, ten, when mother was dead and father was in France and Algeria. How much it meant when he came and took me to France. [They sailed for France on August 25, 1925.] It really saved me."

In France: 1925-1928

The "novelist of Olean" would surely have thought of those years in France in the mid-1920's. St. Antonin, where they settled, was a quaint medieval town. To walk its streets was to return to the Middle Ages. Owen began making plans to build a house there, where he hoped eventually to live with his two sons. Meanwhile, young Tom was sent to a French boarding school, the Lycée Ingres in Montauban, twenty miles southwest of St. Antonin. It was not a happy place for him: He was often lonely and sick. Thirty-six years later, in September 1961, he would write to the late Etta Gullick: "I shall never forget the lycée: its grimness is in my bones" (*The Hidden Ground of Love*, p. 345). The boys were tough and difficult to get along with. But, because life's circumstances forced him to do so, young Tom was learning to adapt to challenging and unpleasant situations. He somehow got involved in the life of the school. Indeed, he became part of a "literary club" of students who wrote novels and critiqued one another's writing. One wonders if the novels he wrote then were autobiography. They surely foreshadow the writing that would be done some years later at Olean.

Even though he had learned to live with the rigors of the Lycée Ingres, it was a joyous day when in May 1928 his father arrived to inform him that they were moving to England. As they drove away from Montauban in a cab, Tom listened to the sound of the horse's hoofs on the road and they said to him: "liberty, liberty, liberty!"

Tom's only regret in leaving France was that they never got to live in the house that Owen was always in process of building, but which he never completed. The two trees Owen planted on his property, one for each of his sons, stood as mute reminders of Owen Merton's unfulfilled desire to be the father that Tom and John Paul needed and that he was never quite able to be. Though of course he could not know it then, time was running out on him. Barely two and a half years later Owen, like Ruth, would be dead of cancer.

In England: 1928-1934

Upon arrival in England, they made their way to Ealing on the outskirts of London and to the home of Owen's aunt, Maud Mary (Grierson) Pearce and her husband, Benjamin Pearce. Tom came to love Aunt Maud with her prim Victorian graciousness. She prepared his wardrobe for him, as once again he went off to boarding school: Ripley Court, a school for young boys in Surrey. It was close enough to Ealing that he could come to Aunt Maud's on weekends. On one occasion they discussed his future. Somewhat hesitantly Tom told her: "I want to be a novelist." She wondered if he would be able to make a living that way. "Perhaps I could be a journalist," he said, "and write for the newspapers."

Some weekends he would spend with his father's younger sister, his aunt Gwyn (Gwynedd Merton Trier) at "Fairlawn" in West Horsley. Tom quickly became friends with his cousins, who were several years younger than he. In fact, he became their favorite visitor, as he organized games for them and read them stories. What is especially intriguing is that some of the stories were written by Tom himself. In December 1993 Dr. Robert Daggy visited Fairlawn and met one of the cousins who showed him four stories written by Tom Merton. They were, as Dr. Daggy observed, "in rather beat-up looking schoolboy notebooks, and all in Merton's handwriting, unmistakable [that is, unmistakably the same as his handwriting in his later life] even in his school days." ⤴

Let us go back, briefly, to the cottage at Olean and the three
authors furiously pounding away at their typewriters, or—
just as likely—sitting around discussing the latest books they
had read or the sad condition of the world in which they
lived. I wonder whether Tom, as he worked on *The Labyrinth*,
might have gone back in memory to those juvenile stories he
had written to entertain his cousins. He probably felt that
they had long ago disappeared, as had other of his very early
writings. Did he perhaps recall the happy Christmas holidays
of 1929, which he spent at Aunt Gwyn's? Did he remember
"The Haunted Castle," a "Winnie the Pooh" story, which he
had written and which he read to his cousins on that
occasion? He surely could not, in his wildest imagination,
have dreamed that sixty-five years after that Christmas
reading, "The Haunted Castle" would be published in *The
Merton Seasonal*, a journal with articles, poems and
bibliographies about himself that has been in publication
since 1976 and is the official organ of the International
Thomas Merton Society.

At Ripley Court

Ripley Court proved a happy experience for young Tom, a
welcome change from the travail of a French lycée. It was at
Ripley Court that formal religious practice became a part of
his life for the first time. It was there that he saw what he had
never seen before: young boys kneeling publicly by their
beds for night prayer. Grace before meals was a new
experience, too; so was Sunday worship, when the boys all
marched off to the parish church, where a transept was
reserved for them. Later he was to refer to these two years at
Ripley as his "religious phase," which, sadly, failed to survive
his years at Oakham.

Vacation in Scotland

As Tom ended his final term at Ripley Court in the summer of 1929, his father decided that they would go to Scotland for the summer to spend some time with friends in Aberdeenshire. They were there but a few days when Owen, obviously ill, announced that he must return to the hospital in London. Tom was to stay for the summer in Scotland. The summer dragged on for him. More and more he withdrew from the family activities to spend his time reading (probably writing, also) and walking in the countryside. He was a lonely young man, but he was discovering, perhaps without realizing it, the peace of solitude. One day he was in the house alone when the phone rang. His first reaction was to let it ring, but finally he picked up the receiver. It was good that he did: It was a telegram message addressed to him. It read: "Entering New York harbor. All well." The telegram was from his father—and came from London. It was obvious to him that his father's mind had snapped: The telegram made no sense except to tell him how very ill his father was.

No one else was in the house. He walked up and down in the silence of the empty room. He was alone, afraid, distraught. He was, after all, only fourteen years old and he was without friends, family, home and now, it seemed, without a father.

Thomas returned at once to Ealing where his uncle Ben informed him: "Your father has a malignant tumor on the brain."

When Thomas visited the hospital, he was surprised and comforted to find his father lucid and intelligible. But there was a large lump on his forehead. Owen would linger for another year and a half.

Oakham School

He had a brain that was bigger than the curriculum.

In the autumn of 1929 at the age of fourteen, young Tom began what was to be a three-year stay as a boarder at

Oakham Public School.[1] The years spent at Oakham were decisive ones in the life of Thomas Merton. During that time he moved from being a clumsy, well-meaning adolescent to a sophisticated (perhaps I should say "pseudo-sophisticated"), worldly young man with cosmopolitan tastes, an increased sense of his own importance, and a strong desire and a firm determination to find his place in the world. It was at Oakham that he earned the reputation of being "something of a rebel."

Oakham School, though small as public schools go in England (the enrollment was about two hundred boys when Merton was there), has a long history. Founded under royal charter from Queen Elizabeth I in 1584, it is one of England's oldest independent schools. The campus is in the center of the market town of Oakham in Rutland, the smallest county in England, amid the charming rolling countryside and thatched cottages of the East Midlands. From London by train through Peterborough it is about ninety miles to Oakham. This meant that, except for long holidays, Tom spent his time in Oakham and its environs.

T. F. Merton, as he signed his name then, proved to be an excellent, even brilliant student. The headmaster, Frank C. Doherty, recognized Tom's unusual abilities and allowed him to add to the normal curriculum of classical studies, additional studies in modern languages and literature. After all, Tom's plans were to prepare for a diplomatic career and modern languages would prove a distinct asset in such a field.

The Debating Team

Tom was much involved in school activities. He was a shrewd and alert member of the debating club. Despite his debating skills, he was more often than not on the losing team. The reason: his independent spirit generally moved him to choose the unpopular side of an issue. Thus, to give but one example, he argued for coeducation at Oakham when the very thought of it was anathema in English public schools. His side lost the debate, though time proved them right, as today Oakham is a school that welcomes young women as well as young men.

Defense of Gandhi

In 1930 the British papers were full of stories about this strange Indian political and spiritual leader, Mohandas Gandhi. In protest against the salt tax, he had led a two-hundred-mile march to extract salt from the sea. He was imprisoned briefly, but was allowed to attend the London Round Table Conference on India. Staid British society was aghast at this strange dark-skinned man with his spindly legs, walking through the fogs of London wearing not much more than a loincloth. They were angry that he had defied British rule.

In the Midlands of England the Oakham schoolboys had also heard of Gandhi, and they too were shocked. One among them, however, argued heatedly that Gandhi and the people of India had a right to invite the British to go home and establish their own home rule. Late one night when the lights were about to be turned out in the dormitory, Tom debated the issue long and intensely with the head prefect. Little did he realize then that years later he would be studying the writings of this man and editing a book of selections from Gandhi on the subject of nonviolence.

Writing at Oakham

During most of his years at Oakham, Tom was involved in the publication of the school paper, *The Oakhamian*, first as a writer, then as editor. Quite a number of articles and poems in the paper for those years carry the signature "T. F. M."

When I visited Oakham in 1985, I was escorted about the campus by John Barber, who had been a classmate of Merton's. We visited the sports facility, fairly recently built. On the walls are wooden plaques listing the rugby teams for various years. The plaque for 1932, Merton's final year at

Oakham, had the names J. Barber and T. F. Merton. Merton was not very good at rugby, Barber told me, but he wanted to be involved.

Visitors From America

In the summer following his first year at Oakham, Sam ("Pop") and Martha Jenkins, Tom's grandparents, and, John Paul, his younger brother, visited him at Oakham. Pop called Tom to his room at the Crown Hotel for a "business meeting." At this meeting he set up a kind of insurance endowment for Tom and for John Paul that ensured that they would have sufficient money for the foreseeable future. Tom was deeply touched by this act of generosity. He was obviously pleased, too, that he no longer would have to worry about money.

The whole family stayed near London most of the summer to be near Owen, whose condition was rapidly worsening. Tom had not seen his father for some time. What he saw—Owen with blurred eyes and an enormous growth on his forehead—filled him with grief and bitterness of spirit. He knew he was soon to lose his father. While Owen had often been an absentee father, Tom knew that he loved his sons and was concerned for them. All he could see was a black void in his future. And he was only fifteen.

From Aunt Maud to Tom Bennett

Since Tom Bennett was Owen's physician, the family saw a good deal of him. Pop was impressed with Bennett and saw him as a good role model for his grandson. Bennett was asked to be Tom's guardian in the event of Owen's death. Further, it was agreed that Tom would now spend his holidays with the Bennetts rather than with Aunt Maud and the other relatives of his father. This suited Pop, who had no special love for Owen's relatives. For young Tom it would mark a big change in his life: moving from the Victorian conservatism and hallowed innocence of Aunt Maud's universe to the more sophisticated and worldly circle of

Bennett's life and friends. From the Bennetts he learned a whole new way of life that he found different and exciting. They introduced him to the avante-garde circle of contemporary writers: Joyce, Hemingway, D. H. Lawrence, Evelyn Waugh and so many others. He brought back to Oakham the vision of another world that most Oakham students knew little or nothing about. His fellow students viewed with a respect bordering on awe the way in which Tom had expanded his horizons. John Barber, when I met him on my visit to Oakham, expressed it in this way: "He had a brain that was bigger than the curriculum."

Discovering the Attraction of Solitude

I just went up there to be there.

Tom returned to Oakham for his second year. Lonely though he was, he plunged himself into school activities. Yet, something was happening in him that he hardly understood: He was beginning to discover another side of his person. This teenager, who on so many occasions had been left alone, began to experience a certain attraction to solitude and quiet time. In his unfinished novel *The Straits of Dover*, which speaks of his life at Oakham, he writes about Brooke Hill, just outside the town: "I liked to go there and think about things by myself." He continues:

I like to be alone on top of [Brooke Hill] and not have to talk to anyone.... I would walk or sit up there for hours, not waiting for anything or looking for anything or expecting anything, but simply looking out over the wide valley, and watching the changes of the light across the hills.... Most of the time I just went up there to be there, to walk around and think.

"I just went up there to be there." Remarkable words about solitude from the lips of a young man not yet eighteen years old. Words with a Zen-like quality, they could well have been penned by a monk at Gethsemani, years later, as he wrote *Thoughts in Solitude* (1958) and "Notes for a Philosophy of

Solitude" which appeared in *Disputed Questions* (1960).

My intention is not to suggest that Tom shunned people. Accompanying his growing sense of the value of solitude was a certain gregariousness. If he loved to be alone, he also loved to be with people. (As he grew older, he would learn that harmonizing these two loves was no easy task. Yet it was a goal he never ceased trying to achieve.) Occasionally he had visitors at Oakham. On one occasion, Tom Bennett and his wife, Iris, came to visit him. Years later, reminiscing—as he so often did in his journals—he speaks of this Sunday visit from Tom and Iris and tells how, after visiting in the park, they went to tea. He mentions also that one of his schoolmates, R. N. Tabacovaci, who was from Hungary, accompanied them.

During the Christmas holidays of 1930, he went—alone—to Strasbourg to study German. While there he experienced something of what was beginning to happen in Nazi Germany. We can be sure that this was on his mind nine years later in the cottage at Olean, as he and the two other young men wrote and reflected on what the war in Europe might mean to them.

Owen Merton's Death

Tom was only a week returned to Oakham after his holiday, when the headmaster summoned him and informed him of the sad news that his father had died. The date was January 18, 1931, just thirteen days before Tom's sixteenth birthday. He was an orphan and he was still very young. He mourned his father's death. But as he eventually distanced himself from the sadness of the event, he came to feel a new sense of independence and rebelliousness. His religious faith was gone. When he went to Sunday chapel (which was compulsory), he kept his mouth tightly closed as the others (some perhaps with no more faith than he had) recited the creed. He no longer believed in God. His one desire, so it seemed, was to be his own person, free from all control and restraints.

Back to America

When the summer term of 1931 was over, young Tom was happy to accept an invitation from his grandparents to come to America. He had not been back to America since he and Owen had left for France in 1925. A month and a half in New York proved a good tonic for him. He went to all the movies he could and bought a number of popular records and a portable phonograph, which he was able to bring back to Oakham. He was a confident young man, as he returned to England, convinced that he knew more than anyone at Oakham, including the headmaster. In his final year he was editor of *The Oakhamian* and welcomed this role as an opportunity to share his thinking with others. He completed his studies at Oakham at the end of 1932.

Rome

> Something I recognized and understood. Something I had been looking for.

On January 31, 1933, Tom's godfather (now his guardian, as well) gave him a birthday party with a gift of a handsome wallet, including tickets and money for a trip to the continent. Eventually he arrived at Rome. As a student of the classics, he naturally turned to the ruins of ancient Rome, the temples, the forum and all the rest. His time in Rome is reported in his autobiography, *The Seven Storey Mountain*, where he describes the sudden attraction he had for the Byzantine mosaics in Christian churches. He was powerfully moved as, for the first time, he felt he had come to know something about this person whom people called Christ. *The Seven Storey Mountain* also tells of a mysterious event that took place in his hotel room in Rome. One night he had a sudden and vivid experience that his father was in the room with him. He began to pray "out of the roots of my life and my being," as he put it.

At the cottage in Olean, Merton worked on his novel, *The Labyrinth*. He wrote of that visit to Rome. He described the spiritual experience he had had there quite differently from the way it was to be told in *The Seven Storey Mountain*. He was strolling, he wrote in *The Labyrinth*, through the ruins of Caligula's palace, and on the wall of the remains of an old church he saw a Byzantine fresco of the crucifixion. "I had often," he wrote, "wandered up and down under the cold and dull brick arches of this palace, hoping to find something interesting, the first time I came to Rome. This, the second time, I had wandered back there, still looking for something: something that would conjure up a banquet of emperors. Instead I found this old church and was suddenly very awed and surprised to find that this was something I recognized and understood. Something I had been looking for" (*The Labyrinth*, unpublished).

Whatever the exact experience may have been, it was a conversion to Christian faith. He bought a copy of the Vulgate, the Latin version of the Bible, and began to read it, probably for the first time in his life. How deep the conversion was is unclear. It was destined not to last. That summer he went once again to America. He brought the Vulgate with him, but showed it to no one. Gradually the Roman experience seemed to fade from his consciousness. When in the fall of 1933, he returned to England to begin his studies at Clare College, Cambridge, he was probably once again an unbeliever.

As he wrote in the Olean cottage in 1939, six years after the "Cambridge Year," surely he looked back with some distress at those disastrous Clare College days. In those days it had been as if he had lost for the time being that sense of peace in solitude. The loneliness that had stalked him all his life had caught up with him. A sense of meaninglessness had set in and led to defiance and rebellion against his better instincts. He had neglected his studies, and had spent too much of his time at pubs. I mentioned earlier the missing pages in *The Labyrinth* that deal with "the party in the middle of the night." His lack of discipline finally had led to disaster for him and for the unknown woman who bore his child. He had been summoned by his guardian, lectured sternly for his undisciplined life and told to return home to America.

We must wonder now if, as he wrote *The Labyrinth* and remembered those painful days, he knew then where the woman was or whether he actually was the father of a child in England. We have no way of knowing. Now, more than sixty years later, it seems that we shall never know for sure.

Columbia University

The place where at last he would find himself.

As we imagine, now, Merton looking about in the cottage at his two friends, Lax and Rice, we also imagine that his emotions must have changed from sorrow at the painful recollection of Cambridge to a joyful remembrance of the many changes that had taken place in his life when he had become a student at Columbia. Columbia had proven to be the place where he would at last find himself. In June 1961, Merton, at that time a monk of Gethsemani, received the University Medal for Excellence from Columbia University. He wrote to President Grayson Kirk: "[M]y response is to acknowledge very heartily the love which I have never ceased to have for Columbia and which has grown with the years.... I have said elsewhere, and I repeat it here, that there is a kind of sanity and magnanimity about Columbia that has a profound importance in the world of today" (*Witness to Freedom*, p. 158).

Of all the happy remembrances he had of the years at Columbia, the most profound was his reception into the Catholic Church on that sixteenth day of November of 1938.

⁓⁓ Back in New York City After Olean, 1939 ⁓⁓

Summer vacation over, the three would-be authors returned to New York City. It was a grim September full of

20

uncertainties. Hitler had invaded Poland. Britain and France had declared war on Germany. The question on many people's minds was: When would America enter the war? In October 1939 Merton enrolled in the Ph.D. program at Columbia. His hope was to write a dissertation on Gerard Manley Hopkins. He never completed the program. ❧

~~~~~~~~~~ *A Franciscan Vocation?* ~~~~~~~~~~

In that same October Merton spoke with Daniel Walsh, the teacher of philosophy, about his future. They were in a downtown hotel drinking a few beers.

"Dan," he said, after some time had passed, "I want to be a priest. I have carried this desire around with me ever since I was baptized. I need to bring it to some resolution."

"I'm not surprised," Dan replied. "From the first time I met you, I was sure that one day you would become a priest."

"Father Ford at Corpus Christi Church thinks I should join the diocesan priests."

"No," Dan said, "I think you're better suited for religious life."

They talked about the Benedictines, the Jesuits, the Trappists. Dan was especially interested in the Trappists, or the Cistercians of the Strict Observance, as they were more properly called. The Trappist life, as Dan described it, seemed too severe to Merton.

Finally Dan said: "Why don't you think of the Franciscans?" (See *The Seven Storey Mountain*, pp. 284-289.)

Merton, who had a fondness for Saint Francis, decided this was a good idea. Dan gave him a letter of introduction to a friend, Father Edmund Murphy, O.F.M., the vocation director who lived at the Church of St. Francis of Assisi on Thirty-First Street. The interview went well and Tom was invited to enter the Franciscan novitiate in August of the following year (1940).

In January 1940 Tom was hired to teach a course in English composition in the extension division of Columbia's

School of Business. At Easter time he visited Cuba. In part, the visit was intended as a pilgrimage to the shrine of Our Lady of Cobre. There he prayed that he might become a priest and promised that his first Mass would be in her honor.

In the summer he returned to Olean and the cottage in the hills. The crowd was larger and noisier that summer and not much writing was done. A good bit of time was spent discussing the Selective Service Act which was before Congress and which was passed in September 1940. Merton, because he was entering a monastery, would not be subject to the draft. Bob Lax and others at the cottage who would be called debated the morality of the law and the right of conscientious objection.

~~~~~~~~~~~~~~~ **Rejection** ~~~~~~~~~~~~~~~

The great stone crucified Christ behind the altar.

Merton was uneasy and restless this summer. He was to enter the Franciscan monastery in August, yet he began to question whether, given his reckless and sinful past, it was right for him to think of becoming a priest. He packed his bag to return to New York.

"Father Edmund doesn't really know me," he kept thinking. "I must tell him everything about myself." He half thought Father Edmund would say: "Forget it. What is past is past."

But Father Edmund did not. He took the matter seriously and told Tom to come back in a few days. Tom pleaded that he could not wait that long. Father Edmund told him to come the next day. He came. The ax fell. Father Edmund told him he should write the provincial and withdraw his application.

Tom was stunned. He went to the Capuchin church across Seventh Avenue. In the confessional he tried to tell his story with much tears and sobs. The confessor decided this was an hysterical young man who certainly did not belong in any monastery. Confirmed in what he did not want to believe, Tom left the confessional. Brokenhearted, the tears running down his cheeks, he buried his face in his hands and prayed before the tabernacle and the great stone crucified Christ behind the altar.

~~~~ Teaching at St. Bonaventure University ~~~~

Devereux Hall: 'Thomas Merton once lived here.'

It was settled: Merton could not be a priest. But he would be as close to being a priest as he could: He bought a set of breviaries at Benziger's and began saying the daily office. If he could not be a Franciscan, he would be as close to them as possible: He sought a teaching job at the Franciscan university in Allegany, New York, St. Bonaventure.

Father Thomas Plassmann, O.F.M., president of the university, gave Merton a kind reception and a job teaching English. Tom would receive forty-five dollars a week together with room and board. His room was in one of the dormitories, Devereux Hall, a big red-brick building in the middle of the campus. Among the things he brought with him were his books, his typewriter and the old portable phonograph he had some years ago brought to Oakham and carried around with him ever since.

Devereux Hall would be his residence from mid-September 1940 to December 9, 1941. Little could he have realized then that fifty-four years later (in June 1995) some five hundred members of the International Thomas Merton Society would gather at St. Bonaventure for its fourth general meeting, and that many on their way to the campus cafeteria would pass Devereux Hall and think with a feeling of awe: "Thomas Merton once lived here."

The course he taught was English 201-202, a survey course designed to give students an appreciation of the best literature and to prepare them for more specialized courses. In a colorful article in *The Merton Seasonal* (summer 1995), Thomas Del Prete has gathered together the remembrances of some of the students whom Merton taught in his year and a half at St. Bonaventure. All those interviewed thought him to be a good teacher, well prepared, who knew "how to get

English literature across to them." He was described as "quiet," with a "wry sense of humor," "a tough but fair marker," "a loner," "thoughtful of his students," someone "we used to have fun with." He enjoyed playing the bongo drums in his room, to the annoyance of some of the residents. "He walked alone on campus. He seemed to walk alone most of the time" (quotations from Thomas Del Prete, "Merton at Bonaventure," *The Merton Seasonal*, summer 1995, pp. 10-12).

～～～～～ Holy Week Retreat at Gethsemani ～～～～～

This is the center of all the vitality that is in America.

During Holy Week in the second semester of his teaching (that is, in the spring of 1941), he made a decision that would change the entire course of his life. He chose to make a retreat at the Cistercian monastery Dan Walsh had told him about: the Abbey of Our Lady of Gethsemani in rural Kentucky, near the town of Bardstown, about fifty miles from Louisville.

The monastery and its liturgy made a deep impression on him. The quiet walks in Surrey when he was at Ripley Court, the aloneness he experienced in Scotland, the sense of "just being there" at Brooke Hill that touched him so deeply at Oakham, indeed, all the many times when he was forced to be alone—all these events seemed, as it were, to lead to and focus on what he was experiencing in this monastery. He loved the silence, the peace. He wondered how he could ever return to the world of busyness and noise. In *The Seven Storey Mountain* he recounts his reflection:

> This is the center of all the vitality that is in America. This is the cause and reason why the nation is holding together....

He goes on to express an understanding of the monastic life about which in his later years he would want to ask questions:

> These men hidden in the anonymity of their choir and their white cowls, are doing for their land what no army, no congress, no president, could ever do as such: they are

winning for it the grace and protection and the friendship of God. (p. 325)

It was love at first sight. That love would be tested, challenged (sometimes by himself), but it would govern the rest of his mortal life.

In the library at the retreat house he discovered a copy of a book by Saint Bernard on the love of God (*De Diligendo Deo*). Saint Bernard entered the Cistercians at Citeaux in France soon after its foundation in 1098. This reformed branch of Benedictines had gone into the forests to live the Benedictine life as strictly as possible. They were having difficulties even surviving till Bernard came with a number of his relatives and infused new life into the struggling group of monks. Bernard became one of the most influential figures of the twelfth century. Sitting in the library at the retreat house, reading this book by Saint Bernard, Merton could never have dreamed that one day he would be compared favorably with Bernard and would, like Bernard, become involved in the dramatic renewal of religious life that would take place in his own time: a renewal that in no small measure he contributed to bringing about.

The day he left Gethsemani he prayed for the grace of a vocation to the Trappist life, if it was God's will. Before the year was over, his prayer would be answered. For some time after his Holy Week retreat he debated whether he should go to Harlem to work for the poor at Friendship House or "give up everything" and go to Gethsemani. One evening in early December 1941 he was walking on the campus grounds near the shrine honoring Saint Therese of Lisieux, whose "little Way" of spirituality he had come to cherish. He prayed to her: "Show me what to do and I will be your priest." All at once, as he prayed, he heard in his imagination, the great bell of Gethsemani ringing in the night. It was about the time the bell for the *Salve Regina* was rung at compline. "The bell," he felt, "seemed to be telling me where I belonged—as if it were calling me home" (*The Seven Storey Mountain*, p. 365).

Finally, he summoned the courage to deal with his past and find out whether or not it constituted an impediment that would prevent his entrance into a monastery or his ordination to the priesthood. After a number of fruitless, hesitant steps to seek clarification, he at last found himself in the office of one of the friars, Father Philotheus Boehner, O.F.M., who assured him that no impediment existed and advised him to apply to Gethsemani. At this point he had to act quickly. The draft board, which had earlier rejected him because of his bad teeth, called him for another examination. He asked for and received an extension of one month, an extension that would become permanent if he entered a religious order.

2. The Monastic Years

~~~~~~~ *A New Life: Gethsemani* ~~~~~~~~

> There is a sense of one's destiny and identity involved in this struggle.

Thus it was that on 9 December 1941, on a wet, slippery night with freezing rain falling, Merton made his way to the railroad station. One of his colleagues on the English faculty, Jim Hayes, saw him to the train. They said their good-byes and Tom Merton began the journey that would change his whole life.

The Abbey of Our Lady of Gethsemani is located in rolling wooded land surrounded by the "Knobs" of Kentucky. Tom did not arrive there till the evening of December 10. He came by train from Louisville to Bardstown, and by taxi from Bardstown to the monastery. The taxi took him into the abbey grounds on a short driveway that makes a sudden left-angle turn leading through a grove of tall trees to the entrance of the gatehouse. The gatehouse today has been replaced by a modern six- or seven-foot wall. In Merton's time the gatehouse was the place where visitors were received. Atop its entrance was a cross and just below it a niche containing a statue of the Virgin Mary. Below the statue and just above the door of the gatehouse was the greeting: *"Pax intrantibus"*—"Peace to all who enter here."

By the time Merton alighted from his taxi, the monks had all retired. He rang the bell and after a long wait, the door was opened by Brother Matthew, the same monk who had let him in at the time of his Holy Week retreat. "Have you come to stay?" Brother Matthew asked. "Yes," Tom answered, "if you will pray for me." The monk assured him that that was what he had been doing.

On that tenth day of December 1941, as he passed into the monastic enclosure, Thomas Merton was just a month and a few days short of his twenty-seventh birthday. He would live exactly twenty-seven years to the day as a monk of Gethsemani, his accidental and unexpected death coming on December 10, 1968.

His first few days were spent in the guest house. Then on December 13, 1941, he was accepted as a postulant by Abbot Frederick Dunne and entered into the life of the monastery. It was like walking into the Middle Ages. The monastery followed a rule that went back to the sixth century: the Rule of Saint Benedict—a rule which the Cistercians of the eleventh century interpreted more strictly than other Benedictines and which the seventeenth-century abbot of the Cistercian Abbey of La Trappe in France, Armand-Jean de Rance, applied even more strictly than the eleventh-century Cistercians. Thus the monks of La Trappe became known as the Cistercians of the Strict Observance or, more informally, as Trappists.

When Merton arrived at Gethsemani, the trappings of modern machinery had not yet made inroads into the life of the monastery. Instead of tractors, they still used horses to plough their fields. They lived in dormitories with little privacy and no central heating. They slept, fully clothed, on straw mattresses supported by four planks. Their meals were meager, to put it mildly: no meat, no fish, no eggs. Dom

Flavian Burns, who entered Gethsemani ten years after Merton, describes something of what life was at Gethsemani at that time: "The food was not that plentiful, but the work was. Eating two pieces of bread and a cup of not quite coffee in the morning and then going down and splitting logs in the winter weather, that was pretty rough" (*Merton: By Those Who Knew Him Best*, p. 105). The monks did not speak to one another; their communication was through sign language. A strange environment indeed for a young man who had "talked himself around the world" and since his Oakham days assumed a pose of heady worldliness. Hardly a place, one would think, for someone who prided himself on being independent. Yet Merton loved every bit of it. He embraced the monastic discipline with the same enthusiasm as he had earlier thrown himself into the disordered, aimless pseudo-freedom of his youth. Entering the monastery was a liberation for him: He was free to become the person God wanted him to be. And in his first enthusiasm he felt assured that what he had to do to fulfill the will of God was to keep the rule of the monastic life. The noisy "rebel" had become the quiet, submissive monk. At least for the time.

To me the great miracle of Merton's life is that he stayed at Gethsemani. That this sophisticated young man with all his worldly interests, not to speak of his undisciplined life heretofore, could accept the rigors of this kind of monastic life and indeed thrive on them is at once proof of the validity of this life-style and a sign of the grace of God operating in this young monk. In 1966, writing to Robert Menchin, who had asked what kind of advice he would give to those who were undergoing a change of career, Merton, while offering some helpful advice, points out that a monastic vocation is distinct from a "career." "In a sense," he said, "you don't pick the monastic vocation, it picks you." He continues:

> In religious terms, that is expressed by saying that one believes oneself "called" by God to live a monastic life. Translated into ordinary language, this refers to a deep implosion which may even go against the grain of one's conscious inclinations. It entails a fight. There is a

considerable amount of doubt and resistance, a great deal of questioning, and at times the whole thing seems absurd. Yet you have to push on with it. There is a sense of one's destiny and identity involved in this struggle. (*Witness to Freedom*, p. 255)

He goes on to make a statement about the stability of his own vocation: "I have never for a moment questioned the vocation to be a monk, but I have had to settle many other questions about ways and means, the where and the how of being a monk" (Ibid.).

We must remember this was a statement made in 1966. It may be doubted whether the young monk just getting inured to the monastic life would have spoken, or even thought, in just this way. But it is helpful for us to read it now as a kind of prophetic statement of what was to come in the life of this not-so-ordinary monk. The "rebel" streak was dormant; but, Merton being who he was, it was bound to emerge sooner or later. Yet, as we shall see, it would be not destructive, but creative: It would help to open up new and fresh ways of understanding monastic life in our time. More than that, it would be instrumental in opening up new ways (or perhaps, better, forgotten ways) of a lived spirituality that would be, not just for monks, but for all women and men who seek to live a life of deeper interiority.

～ A. Merton's Monastic Life Before the Publication of ～ The Seven Storey Mountain

The daily schedule followed by the monks was very different from that of the three friends in Olean. The monks rose at 2:00 a.m. (Often this would have been the time the Olean group would be going to bed!) They had half an hour of personal prayer at 2:30. Then the lights went on and vigils (the canonical offices of matins and lauds), made up of twenty psalms, some canticles and some readings, were sung. Vigils would be over at 4:00 a.m. At that time the priest-monks would say their private Masses assisted by one of the other monks. The rest would go to a communion Mass. Then came fifteen minutes of thanksgiving. Next the monks had time for personal prayer till 5:30 a.m., when they would return to the chapel for the canonical hour[2] of prime. After prime they gathered for chapter, where the abbot would speak to them, generally on the Rule, and transact any necessary business that involved the monks. The monks would next go to the dormitory to make their beds and then to the refectory for a cup of coffee and two slices of dry bread.

After breakfast, there was an hour for reading. This was precious time for Merton: Among other things, he read the early Fathers of the Church as well as the Cistercian Fathers of the eleventh century. These texts, for the most part, were in Latin. Merton, being fluent in Latin, had no difficulty in reading them. The Greek Fathers, however, he had to read in the Latin translation. He regretted that he had not taken the study of Greek more seriously when he was at Oakham!

At 7:45 a.m. the monks returned to the chapel for the office of terce, then there would be the daily high Mass (no one receiving the Eucharist, as they had done so earlier!). Mass completed, they would have the office of sext and then engage in two hours of manual labor. This was Merton's schedule in the beginning, but very soon, in place of the manual labor, he was given this time for writing. After the morning work, the monks were back in chapel for the examen of conscience. Dinner followed, the one meal where they could eat as much as they wanted, though the choice of food was quite limited. Potatoes and bread were the staples. Generally there were soup and some vegetables. After dinner there was the office of none, followed by a period of rest. After siesta there would be two more hours of work in the afternoon. Vespers would be at 4:30 p.m. After a period of quiet prayer, they would have a collation (a small meal). After dishes were done they would assemble for compline, the final office of the day. Compline concluded with the singing of the *Salve Regina*, after which the monks received the abbot's blessing and then they were off to bed.

I said earlier that the great miracle of Merton's story is

that, with the background from which he came, he stayed a monk of Gethsemani to the very end. But I think of a second miracle, namely, the fact that, given the highly structured life I have just described (which gave him very limited time for reading and writing), Merton nevertheless was able to produce the staggering amount of writing (books, poetry, letters, journals) that leaped out from his old banged-up typewriter.

The Letter to Father Abbot

Soon after Merton's entrance into the novitiate, Father Robert McGann, the novice-master, suggested that Tom write a letter to the abbot, Dom Frederic Dunne, explaining his conversion experience and naming the various places where he had lived. The letter was written on January 22, 1942. (See *The School of Charity*, pp. 5-7.) The letter is something of a summary-outline of what he would later flesh out in his autobiography, *The Seven Storey Mountain*. This letter may well have put in Father Abbot's mind the idea that this unusual novice should one day write the story of his life prior to the time of his entrance into the monastery.

In 1944 Merton, or Frater Louis (to use his name in religious life), was allowed to make temporary vows. At this time he was obligated to make a will for the three years that would precede his final vows. One item in this will sheds some light on his past: the bequest made to his guardian Thomas T. Izod Bennett "to be paid by him to the person mentioned to him by me in my letters, if that person can be found" (*The School of Charity*, p. 8). This statement indicates his concern to take responsibility for his past; it also seems to close the question: Did Merton himself know where "that person" could be located?

Merton made his temporary vows on the feast of St. Joseph, March 1944. On March 6 Frater Louis wrote to the abbot of his desire to surrender completely to God and offer himself for three intentions: for peace, for his brothers in the monastery and for the salvation of those in the world with whom he was associated in his "sinful life." Soon after this event, Merton would have begun his studies for the priesthood. He would have studied the same basic texts used in seminaries around the world: texts heavily based on neo-scholasticism at its worst. (I speak as one who knows, one who studied these same texts at about the time Merton was required to deal with them.) These texts influenced his writing for only a brief time, after which he turned in his writing to a methodology of experience that was more appropriate and natural for him.

~.~ B. Merton's Monastic Life After the Publication of ~.~ The Seven Storey Mountain

But before his ordination to the priesthood (which took place on May 26, 1949, the feast of the Ascension, with several of his Columbia friends present), an event occurred that would change the course of his monastic career. His autobiography, *The Seven Storey Mountain*, which the abbot (Dom Frederic Dunne) had directed him to write, was published October 4, 1948, and became an instant best-seller. It sold 600,000 copies the first year and literally millions of copies in various languages have continued to sell since then.[3] The young man who had gone to Gethsemani to find peace and solitude suddenly became a public figure in the world he thought he had left behind. Fan mail poured into Gethsemani: Much of it, especially in the early years, was simply adulatory and could be answered with a form letter of thanks signed by Father Louis. But as time went on some of the correspondence became more substantive and called for more than a form letter. Thus began the Merton correspondence that includes more than 4,000 letters, most of which have been published in five volumes. (These volumes are identified in Chapter Four.)

Art and Contemplation

The many letters he wrote were in addition to the many

books, essays and poems he produced during his years in the monastery. Some of these will be discussed later in this book. What I want to deal with at this point is the problem (or pseudo-problem) his writing posed for him. When he first entered the monastery, he expected he would not be allowed to write. And he was convinced (at least he *thought* he was) that he ought not to write. After all, he had come to the monastery to be a contemplative. A contemplative, as he put it early in his monastic career, enters into God in order to be created, whereas the writer enters into himself in order to create. (See *Seeds of Contemplation*, p. 71.) He had to make a choice, so he thought, between Thomas Merton the writer and Frater Louis, the contemplative. Yet, he so desperately wanted to write. It was almost as if he *had* to write, as if ink flowed in his veins and he had to be bled of it regularly.

Happily, Merton's superiors recognized this young monk's gifts and ordered him to write. Though he continued to struggle with the problem, he reminds himself that his writing is "disinfected" by obedience. It took him a long time to see his writing as a help to his contemplation instead of its rival. His superiors were wise men. Had Merton been forced to stop writing he would have shriveled up as a monk, perhaps even left the monastery. God does not give gifts for us to throw them away. Moreover, if Merton had persisted in believing (if he ever really believed it) that were he to use his gift as a writer he could not be a contemplative, his most important message for the contemporary world would have been muted. For if one cannot be both a contemplative and a writer, it would follow that one could not be both a contemplative and a housewife, a contemplative and a truck driver, a contemplative and a teacher, a contemplative and a worker on the assembly line.

Merton's personal problem thus highlights a problem of universal significance. The fact that he finally came to see that contemplation could be for anyone—this is what made him and continues to make him one the most important spiritual influences of our century and perhaps of centuries to come. That he eventually came to this confident assurance was, I believe, a result not of his reading (for no one at that time was writing this sort of thing), but from his own experience of contemplation.

Contemplation and Solitude

Yet another problem Merton faced when he became a monk—a problem that persisted to his life's end—had to do with what might be called the "locale" of contemplation. If he saw a conflict between writing and contemplation, he also saw a close affinity between contemplation and the amount of solitude available to a would-be-contemplative.

I should point out that, enamored though he was of Gethsemani, it was actually his second choice. Had he been able to do so, he would have joined the Carthusians, who lived as hermits, each with his separate hermitage. But in 1941, there were no Carthusian monasteries in the United States (the first American Charterhouse was established in Vermont in the early 1950's), and there was no possibility of entering one in Europe because of the war.

Merton's agitation for solitude became more insistent after Dom James Fox became abbot of Gethsemani. A graduate of Harvard Business School, Dom James considerably modernized the abbey. The noise of machinery, the busyness of life at Gethsemani, only spurred Merton's determination to ask for transfer to a monastery with a more eremetical type of existence. He received no encouragement from his abbot or his confessor. They insisted he was in the right place: God wanted him at Gethsemani. The story of his early struggle for a more solitary existence is detailed in the journal he named *The Sign of Jonas*. Like Jonas, he heard God calling him in one direction, while he wanted to go in another.

Dom James solved the problem—for a time at least. He gave Merton the use of an old tool shed out in the woods and allowed him to spend time there each day. The year was 1953. Merton was ecstatic: At last, he said, I have what I have been waiting for and looking for all my life. He called this hermitage St. Anne's. It was while he was there that he wrote *Thoughts in Solitude*. It would not be till 1965 that he would be given permission to live as a full-time hermit on the grounds of the monastery—and in a much more adequate hermitage than a discarded tool shed.

Novice Master—Contemplative of Compassion

In 1955 Dom James showed his confidence in Father Louis: He appointed him to the very important position of master of novices. Merton brought a breath of fresh air into the novitiate at a time when it was overflowing with novices. He continued in this position for ten years and left on these many young monks the stamp of his own thinking about monasticism at a time when his understanding of what it meant to be a monk was undergoing radical changes. The rebel streak, buried at the entrance of Gethsemani when he first arrived, was beginning to resurface.

Between 1955 and 1965 Merton became a very different kind of monk from the one who had in 1941 entered Gethsemani with the fervent desire to leave the world behind and give himself to God alone. One of the things going on in him was the maturing realization, born of his contemplation, that it is not possible to leave the world in any real sense. There is simply no place else to go. The world is on both sides of the monastic walls: Monks face the same fundamental human problems that all men and women have to deal with. They also have responsibilities to the world.

This dawning intuition was given classical expression in what has come to be known as "the Vision of Louisville." On March 18, 1958, Merton was in Louisville on an errand for the monastery. Standing at the corner of Fourth and Walnut Streets, he had an experience which may well be described as "mystical." He saw people hurrying in and out of stores in a shopping district. Suddenly he was overwhelmed with a realization that he loved all these people and that they were neither alien to nor separate from him. The experience challenged the concept of a separate "holy" existence lived in a monastery. He experienced the glorious destiny that comes simply from being a human person and from being united with, not separated from, the rest of the human race. Here are Merton's words:

> I was suddenly overwhelmed with the realization that I loved all those people, that they were mine and I theirs.... It was like waking from a dream of separateness, of spurious self-isolation in a special world, the world of renunciation and supposed holiness. The whole illusion of a separate holy existence is a dream. (*Conjectures of a Guilty Bystander*, p. 156)

"This sense of liberation from an illusory difference," he goes on to say, "was such a relief and such a joy that I almost laughed out loud. And I suppose my happiness could have taken form in the words: '...[T]hank God that I *am* like other men [and women].'"

His reflection on the experience enabled him to see that in some mysterious way his monastic solitude belonged to all these people.

> I have a responsibility for it in their regard, not just in my own. It is because I am one with them that I owe it to them to be alone, and when I am alone they are not "they," but my own self. There are no strangers! (Ibid., p. 158)

He continues his reflection on the splendor of it all:

> Then it was as if I suddenly saw the secret beauty of their hearts, the depths of their hearts, where neither sin nor desire nor self-knowledge can reach, the core of their reality, the person that each one is in God's eyes. If only they could all see themselves as they really *are*. If only we could see each other that way all the time. There would be no more war, no more hatred, no more greed. (Ibid.)

This experience, while occurring outside the monastery, took place, I believe, because of what had been going on inside this monk during the seventeen years he had lived in the monastery. During those years Thomas Merton had indeed become a contemplative. Contemplation taught him, as it must teach any true contemplative, that in finding God he had found God's people and he had found them in God.

More and more in the late fifties and in the sixties, Merton was in touch with people outside the monastery—especially those committed to the struggle for peace and for civil rights. The monastic walls, figuratively at least, came tumbling down, as Merton reached out to people who sought his counsel and wanted to listen to the wisdom he could share with them.

This kind of contact with people posed for Merton what was to be perhaps the most important question for him in the sixties. It was not the question: Do I as a monk have the right to reach out to these people? Nor was it the question: Should I leave the monastery and join them in their struggle? No, the question he knew he had to deal with was: What does it mean for me to be in the monastery *for people*? He was convinced that God wanted him in the monastery. He was, by the sixties, equally convinced that his monastic life did not absolve him from the duty of accepting his share of responsibility for the problems (war, racism, poverty, prejudice) that existed in the world. He realized, too, that we do not choose our own problems. They are thrust upon us by the times in which we live. In 1962 he wrote to a correspondent in Brazil: "We have got to try to solve the problems of our own countries while at the same time recognizing our higher responsibility to the whole human race.... [Y]et, I remain a contemplative." He sees no contradiction: "[F]or I think at least some contemplatives must try to understand the providential events of the day. God works in history, therefore a contemplative who has no sense of history, no sense of historical responsibility, is not fully a Christian contemplative" (*The Hidden Ground of Love*, pp. 186-187).

Contemplation, in other words, sparked compassion. The monastic choice (indeed the Christian choice) is not God or the world. Rather, it is both. It is all-in-one. It is an acceptance of the unity of all reality in the ground of love in which all things find their identity and their uniqueness. We are distinct from one another and God, but we are not separate from God or from one another.

How Merton's compassionate concern for the world played itself out in his life and in his writings will be detailed in later chapters.

Merton the Hermit

In 1965 Thomas Merton shattered Trappist tradition: He became the first American Trappist to be allowed to live by himself as a hermit. On the feast of Saint Bernard, August 20, 1965, in the fiftieth year of his life, Thomas Merton headed for the cinder block building in the woods on the monastery grounds. Originally constructed for ecumenical dialogue, it was to be his hermitage. Before departing he gave a talk in the novitiate. It was lighthearted, jovial. He tried to work up a tear, he said, but just could not. "The general impression I get," he tells them, "is that people are saying: 'Well good old Louie, he made it anyhow.'"

In the midst of a lot of good-natured humor, he spells out in a thoughtful way the meaning of the hermit life as a "life without care": a life free from worry and anxiety, because life is in God's hands. If God takes care of the birds and the flowers, surely then God will take care of us also. To be free of care is not to be free from responsibility, from the concern we must have for the poor, the oppressed and the marginalized in society. It is just that our care becomes a participation in God's care for all the creatures God made.

Once he had settled in at the hermitage, he sent a copy of his daily schedule to the abbot.

2:15 a.m. rise; Lauds; meditation till 5:00; breakfast; Lectio [reading of Scripture] till 7:30; then Prime and rosary; 8:00 manual work, chores, etc.; 9:30 terce, sext, none.

Then to the monastery for private Mass, followed by thanksgiving and part of the psalter; dinner in infirmary refectory.

Then return to hermitage; siesta or light reading; vespers at 1:00, followed by meditation; 2:15 writing, work or walk;

4:15 vigils anticipated. 5:00 supper, followed by compline;
6:00 New Testament, meditation, examen; 7:00 retire.
(Unpublished note to Dom James)

Thomas Merton had finally achieved what he had been
longing for ever since he had come to Gethsemani. Writing to
Naomi Stone, he says: "[T]he five days I have been here all
the time have been simply perfect, and everything seems to
indicate it will go on that way, but of course the original joy
of it will doubtless wear off but for one thing I have no
doubts: this is exactly right for me. It is all that I ever hoped
for and more" (*Witness to Freedom*, p. 146). He tells Dom
Jacques Winandy: "I have rapidly discovered that what I am
seeking [here] is not eremitism or spirituality or
contemplation but simply God" (*The School of Charity*, p. 290).

A small book (first published in a South American
journal), *Day of A Stranger*, describes a day in the hermitage.
In whimsical, bewitching prose Merton takes pride in his
growing affinity with nature. He and the birds form an
ecological balance. Like Saint Francis he preaches to the
birds: "Esteemed friends, I have no message for you except
this: be what you are: be *birds*."

As he sees a warplane flying low "with a scientific egg in
its breast," he muses that living in the woods is a reminder
that he is free not to be a number, that it is still possible to
make a choice. After all, he says:

> This is not a hermitage—it is a house ("Who was that
> hermitage I seen you with last night?...") What I wear is
> pants. What I do is live. How I pray is breathe.... If you see
> a meditation going by, shoot it.... Spiritual life is guilt. Up
> here in the woods is seen the New Testament, that is to say,
> the wind comes through the trees and you breathe it.

The three years in the hermitage were some of the most
memorable in Merton's life. If he formed an ecological
balance with the birds, he also achieved something of an
intellectual balance with the many people who came to his
hermitage, sometimes through their writings, sometimes
through personal visits. I shall name but a few of his visitors:

French philosopher Jacques Maritain, Chilean poet Nicanor Parra, Nicaraguan priest Ernesto Cardenal, lifelong advocate of nonviolence Hildegard Goss Mayr, popular folksinger Joan Baez, Vietnamese poet in exile Thich Nhat Hanh. And there were others. Perhaps too many for one who had chosen to live the solitary life.

More and more during this period he turned to literary reflections: on Latin American poets, William Faulkner's novels, Flannery O'Connor's works, the writings of the French existentialist Albert Camus, to mention but a few.

St. Joseph's Hospital—Louisville, 1966

On March 25, Merton went to St. Joseph's Hospital in Louisville for back surgery.[4] A few days after the operation a young student nurse came to care for him. First resenting her for interfering with his reading, his attitude quickly changed: He began to look forward to her coming. Before he knew it, he had fallen in love with her and she with him. The story of this love—with Merton's scheming to meet her, his efforts to reach her on the phone, the letters he wrote her and the poems—covers several months. It was a time of joy and happiness for Merton, but also one of anxiety, fear—hardly the "life without care" he had spoken about not too many months earlier. Some of his friends who knew what was going on could not believe it. They were concerned, at times angry, at times wondering if he had taken leave of his senses. It was an episode in his life which showed his vulnerability and his humanness. In his relationship with God, as I have pointed out earlier, he had more and more come to trust his experience. Now, perhaps for the first time, he was trusting his experience in a genuine relationship with another human person.

What that experience showed him was that he could love and be loved. And that surely is something quite wonderful for a person who felt the need to write: "As an orphan, I went through the business of being passed around from family to family, and being a 'ward,' and an 'object of charitable concern,' etc. etc. I know how inhuman and frustrating that can be—being treated as a thing and not as a person" (*The Hidden Ground of Love*, p. 605). At last he had discovered a relationship in which he was loved as a person and was able to return that love. It is hard to believe that this was not a good experience for Merton; it is not hard, however, to realize that, given his monastic commitment and his need to be a hermit, this relationship inevitably would be short-lived. It was terminated by the end of the summer of 1966. Whether it was a good experience for M., the young student nurse, is quite another question, one that only she can answer; and, understandably, it has been her choice to maintain her privacy.

As I wrote in *Silent Lamp: The Thomas Merton Story*, "One can ask the question—though without trying to suggest an answer one way or another—whether Merton treated her fairly and honestly when he must have known that, when the moment came that he had to make a choice, he would choose his hermitage. One of the verses in *Eighteen Poems*, which he wrote for her...has a poignant stanza that embodies the helpless yearning for a love that could not be."[5]

> If only you and I
> Were possible.
> (*Eighteen Poems*, New York: New Directions, 1985)

Thomas Merton had learned from experience what he had written about in a more speculative tone in 1961: "The vocation to charity is a call not only to love but to *be loved*. The man who does not care at all whether or not he is loved is ultimately unconcerned about the true welfare of the other and of society. Hence we cannot love unless we also consent to be loved in return" (*The New Man*, p. 91).

Merton's Ecumenical Interests and His Asian Journey

By the 1960's Merton had become strongly ecumenical in his reading and thinking. But his understanding of ecumenism was not so much resolving doctrinal differences as finding areas of unity among various religious traditions. He had a special kinship with the Abrahamic religions that traced their origins to Abraham: Judaism, Christianity and Islam. He was in touch with Jewish writers such as Abraham Heschel, Zalman Schachter, Eric Fromm and others. His correspondence with the famous Christian Arabic scholar, Louis Massignon, put him in contact with Sufism, the mystical strain in Islam.

His interest in Zen was deeply earnest and of long standing. He was in touch with the noted Zen master, D. T. Suzuki, reading his books and meeting him briefly in New York City in 1964. He was attracted also to Chinese religions, especially Taoism, an attraction that led to one of his most delightful books of poetry, *The Way of Chuang Tzu*.

And, finally, of course, there was the great adventure that began with ecstatic joy and ended in such grim tragedy: the visit in 1968 to Asia. In 1968 Merton wrote to Dom Jean Leclercq that he would be delighted to speak at the AIM [Inter-Monastic Aid] meeting that was to be held in Bangkok, Thailand. He expressed his conviction that it was important for him to meet some eastern monks and also some of the Christian monks in Asia. Dom Flavian Burns, the newly elected abbot of Gethsemani, was at first reluctant to give the necessary permission. But by early summer he had been persuaded to do so and Merton began making plans for the face-to-face meeting with the Asia he had visited so many times in his writings and in his imagination.

The story of his visit to Asia is set forth in *The Asian Journal*, which will be discussed later in more detail. In Chapter Four I shall highlight four significant events of that visit: his talk at Calcutta, his trip to Dharamasala to meet the Dalai Lama, his visit to Polonnaruwa, and his final talk and tragic death in Bangkok, Thailand.

Together with the monks from Asia, whom he had come to address, Merton was staying at the Red Cross Camp in Bangkok. On December 10, 1968, the twenty-seventh anniversary of his entrance into Gethsemani, Merton gave the talk he had come halfway around the world to give. The talk was entitled: "Marxism and Monastic Perspectives." He was televised for the first time, as he gave that talk. The talk, somewhat rambling, yet full of helpful insights, did not make much of an impression on his listeners at the time. He was scheduled to answer questions about it that evening. But he never made that session. That afternoon he died an accidental death. No one was with him at the time. He was found late in the afternoon lying on the floor of the cottage he occupied, with a large electric fan lying on top of him and deep burns in the area of his side and groin. It may have been a heart attack and a vain effort to steady himself by grabbing the fan. More probably, he was electrocuted, perhaps by a faulty wiring in the fan.

Thus it was that on the twenty-seventh anniversary of his monastic life, he went home, not to Gethsemani, but to the many-mansioned paradise that he had caught glimpses of in his contemplation, but which he now possesses forever.

The same day, December 10, 1968, the distinguished Protestant theologian Karl Barth died. In *Conjectures of a Guilty Bystander* (p. 12), Merton had commented on a dream Karl Barth had written about. The great theologian was very fond of Mozart's music and every day, before going to work on his huge Church Dogmatics, he listened to a Mozart piece. One day he had a dream in which he was appointed to examine Mozart on his theology. Deliberately he centered his questions about the Mozart Masses. But Mozart refused to answer a single question. Barth came to understand that Mozart was not a theologian and that it was not a theologian who spoke through music. Instead, he tells us: "it is a Child, even a divine Child, who speaks to us in Mozart's music." Merton comments on Barth's dream:

> Fear not, Karl Barth! Trust in the divine Mercy. Though you have grown up to be a theologian, Christ remains a child in you. Your books (and mine) matter less than we might think! There is in us a Mozart who will be our salvation.

Barth had written that if he ever got to heaven, he would "first seek out Mozart and only then inquire after Augustine,

St. Thomas, Luther, Calvin and Schleieriermacher" (Karl Barth, *Wolfgang Amadeus Mozart* [Grand Rapids, Mich.: Eerdmans, 1986], p. 16). On that tenth day of December 1968, Merton may well have accompanied him on such a visit.

Notes

[1]The term "public" is deceiving for American readers. English public schools were actually privately-endowed institutions.

[2]The daily prayer of the monks comprised a number of hours: matins, lauds, prime, terce, sext, none, vespers and compline. "Hour" in this usage does not mean a 60-minute period of time. Prime, terce, sext, none and compline lasted about ten minutes each. Lauds (morning prayer) and vespers (evening prayer) were about a half-hour. Matins was a bit longer.

[3]For a further discussion of *The Seven Storey Mountain* and its reception, see Chapter Four.

[4]This material is similar to my description of this episode in *Silent Lamp* (pp. 200-201). Merton's detailed account of his relationship with M. is told in volume 6 of the journals, *Learning to Love: Exploring Solitude and Freedom*, edited by Christine M. Bochen, which is scheduled for publication in late 1997.

[5]William H. Shannon, *Silent Lamp: The Thomas Merton Story* (New York: Crossroad, 1992), p. 200.

CHAPTER TWO

Is Merton for Today or Is He Passé?

*The intent of this book is to introduce Thomas Merton to you,
the reader, to invite you to embark on the adventure of
reading his works and to suggest ways of approaching his
writings.*

The previous chapter was a relatively brief introduction to
the man and his life. Subsequent chapters will deal with
some of the following topics: what to look for in Merton's
works (prominent themes you will find there), where to
begin in reading his writings and how to evaluate his works
(obviously some are better than others). In this chapter I shall
try to make attractive to you the invitation I extend to begin
reading Thomas Merton (or to continue reading him if you
are already doing so, or to return to Merton if you were once
a Merton reader and are one no longer). It is essential that I
do this. For today there is so much literature available that
readers, since they cannot read everything, must of necessity
be choosy in what they read. This tells me that if I want you
to read Merton, I have to offer you reasons that will be
sufficiently convincing to persuade you to make this choice.

I want to anticipate a question that may be forming (or
already has formed) in the minds of some who, years ago,
may have dabbled in Merton's works, but who read them no
more, or who may remember their parents or aunts or uncles
talking enthusiastically about Merton, but who never got

around to reading him themselves. Such a person might be inclined to say: "I read Thomas Merton's writings in the late 1940's and in the 1950's, or I heard about him later. But let's face it: Merton wrote on his old beat-up typewriter. He knew nothing of computers. He never had the chance of surfing the World Wide Web. Today we have all these new ways of communicating. Besides, we are on the verge of entering into a new millennium far removed from Merton's world of the mid-twentieth century. What possible reasons could I have for reading Merton today? Granted that he once was 'in,' but isn't he 'out' now? Isn't his stuff outdated? Will he have meaning for people heading into a new century?"

That is a forceful and timely question! If I cannot give you a reason for reading Merton today, there is not much point in my continuing with this book. The assumption behind your question seems, at first hearing, to make a good deal of sense. Thomas Merton died nearly thirty years ago (1968) and he was a monk. In any generation only a handful of authors produce writings that long survive their author's death. One might well expect that a monk's writings, which presumably would appeal only to a limited audience, would more than likely go with him into the grave.

Merton's Continuing Popularity

Yet this has not happened to Merton's writings. They are still very much "in." Recently, I visited a large secondhand book store in a large city in the Midwest. It carried books in almost every area, with an exceptionally large number of books in the areas of philosophy and religion. I asked the proprietor: "Of all the books you sell in so many different areas, who are the authors most asked for?" He answered: "C. S. Lewis, Friedrich Nietzsche and Thomas Merton." An interesting trio, wouldn't you say?

Now, unquestionably, Merton was a unique monk. One would have to go all the way back to the twelfth century—to Saint Bernard—to find a monk whose writings were as influential as Merton's have been. Merton had a wide readership in his lifetime, and it was not primarily monastic. In fact, I would venture the perhaps surprising opinion that laypeople took to his writings more than monks did. There were monks who were skeptical about the things he said or even about the areas in which he chose to write. A lot of lay folk, on the other hand, chose to forget that he was a monk and felt that he was addressing them in their own circumstances of life. Figuratively, they took him out of the monastery and made him one of their own.

The remarkable fact is that, even though close to thirty years have passed since Merton's death, his readership has grown steadily. His writings continue to spark interest. Reprinted year after year, translated into many different languages, they are read by countless numbers of people in many parts of the world. It's as if there is a kind of magic about the name of Thomas Merton that brings together people of many diverse backgrounds.

New Merton materials are continually bursting into publication. Between 1985 and 1994 five hefty volumes of Merton's letters were published. Once the publication of the letters was completed, there appeared, in 1995, the first of a projected series of seven volumes of Merton journals. January 1996 saw the publication of volume two, and the plan is to issue the remaining volumes every six months, which means that by 1998 all the journals will have been published. The publication of the letters and the journals has added and will continue to add immeasurably more to our knowledge of Merton than we could learn about him from his published works. I say this because in both the letters and the journals one finds an intimacy and a sense of freedom that are not always so clearly evident in his published writings. The reason is obvious: In these more personalized writings, he did not have to write with one eye to censors looking over his shoulder. With the published works it was quite different: He had more than his share of bouts with the censors who all too frequently questioned the truth or the propriety of what he wrote. The latter was especially a problem for them. They tried to keep this sometimes recalcitrant monk from writing anything that, in their estimation, would disedify readers or bring criticism on the Order.

Besides his own extensive publications, a large body of literature has grown up about Thomas Merton. People from different academic backgrounds have written extensively about the man and his books. There are several biographies, numerous books about his writings and the themes that may be found in them. Over two hundred dissertations have explored his thought. Frequent journal articles analyze different aspects of his writing; there are two journals specifically devoted to Merton Studies: *The Merton Seasonal* (which is the official publication of the International Thomas Merton Society) and *The Merton Annual*. I would not want to say that everything that has been written about him is worthwhile or even fair to him. It is a sad fact that too much of it is poor writing and not representative of his thought. But with so much being written about him, this is almost inevitable. And, of course, very good things have been written which have given deeper insight into the world of Thomas Merton.

In colleges and universities students in increasing numbers register for Merton classes. People meet at Merton societies, conferences and lectures. In 1997 the International Thomas Merton Society celebrated its tenth anniversary with its fifth general meeting held in Mobile, Alabama. Previous meetings were held in various parts of the country: Louisville, Kentucky (1989); Rochester, New York (1991); Colorado Springs, Colorado (1993); Allegany, New York (1995). There are some twenty-five chapters of the International Thomas Merton Society. They meet on a regular basis and exist throughout the United States, as well as in Belgium and England. In 1996 the Russian Thomas Merton Society came into existence in Moscow.

Perhaps at this point you may say: "OK, I am impressed by what you say about Merton's prodigious output and his unwaning and even growing popularity. But, frankly, I am not content to do what others do just because they do it. So I need to know some of the reasons why Merton and his writings are attracting so many people today. What do they find in him that is so contemporary?"

His Humanness

Fair enough. Let me try to suggest some possible answers. What I would want to say first is that Merton was so genuinely human. He was real. He detested phoniness and pretense. He said what he thought and tried to mean what he said. In him we find an earnest, genuine, no-holds-barred human being struggling, like the rest of us, to find meaning, seeking to confront the absurdity that life so often appears to be. He knew loneliness, homelessness and alienation. To one of his correspondents he wrote that some people think that going into a monastery is the same as going into nirvana. Not so, he says, there is work to be done, there are decisions to be made, and many questions yet to be answered.

He was human in his strengths, but also in his weaknesses. His clay feet are there for us to see. Like ourselves he had attachments he had to rid himself of and illusions he had to unmask. He was vulnerable in his humanness: a reality he never tried to hide or deny. Deeply committed to his monastic vocation, he often lamented the petty infidelities that seemed to belie that commitment. So much of him was so much like what we all are.

His Ability to Articulate the Human Condition

One of the precious human gifts he had, which most of us lack and which makes him different from us, was the ability to articulate the human situation and the struggles of mortals to deal with the ambiguities, the contradictions, the inequities which life often thrusts upon us. This gift of communicating clearly and wisely makes it possible for so many diverse people (not just in one country, but in many) to identify with him. They read his story and they see something of their own story in it. They read his reflections on life and what he says so often strikes responsive chords in their lives. He gives voice to thoughts and intuitions that were in their minds and hearts, but which they did not know were there, till Merton gave them expression. He speaks not just to us, but oftentimes for us. He was able to see the real issues at stake before others even began to look for them. So often in reading him, one reflects: "Yes, that's the way I feel," or "That's what I want to be," or "Right, he has hit on the issues that matter to me."

He wrote with wit, but also with wisdom. He once wrote an essay entitled "Christian Culture Needs Oriental Wisdom" (appearing as "Love and Tao" in *Mystics and Zen Masters*, pp. 69-80). I suggest Christian culture needs a bit of the wisdom Merton can offer, too. He was able to see and articulate the real deep-down issues of life which we need to deal with and struggle with. At the same time, he was a happy person and a man of hope. Joy ran deep in him. Life and faith and love were wondrous gifts never to be taken for granted.

Reverence for People

People were precious to him: He respected their uniqueness. One need only read his many letters to see how he makes every effort to identify with others and find common ground on which they can comfortably meet. He was convinced that the ultimate ground in which we all meet is that "Hidden Ground of Love" we call God. God can be named in many ways, yet God always remains mystery that no words of ours can ever grasp. To Merton the name of preference was Mercy. "God," he wrote, "is like a calm sea of mercy" (*Seasons of Celebration*, p. 120). In the wonderful conclusion of *The Sign of Jonas*, he has God speak: "I have always overshadowed Jonas with My mercy.... Have you had sight of Me, Jonas My child? Mercy within mercy within mercy" (p. 362). For many people, brought up with the notion of a God who is judge, rewarding and punishing almost unfeelingly, approaching the divine as mystery of mercy can be a source of light and joy.

Not only does he seek common ground with those to whom he relates, he responds to people in their uniqueness. Thus, his letters to Dorothy Day, for instance, have quite a different tone from those he wrote to Daniel Berrigan. He was at once strong and gentle in his relationships. Victor Stier, an American government official who was his host in Sri Lanka, wrote to the late Wilbur H. Ferry[1] that Merton made a tremendous impression on him. As they discussed Buddhism, Stier soon learned that Merton was much better informed about this religious tradition than he was. Merton disagreed with him when he expressed the opinion that Buddhism was a negative approach to life. But, Stier says of him, "He was surprisingly gentle in disagreement, he had a wonderful way about him." A shrewd observation with which hundreds of his correspondents would express wholehearted agreement. ❧

Bursting the Bonds of Cultural Limitation

Merton was a person of cosmopolitan tastes and interests. He was very much at home in the American Catholic tradition (which, in many ways, he helped to form), but, unlike so many other writers in the field of spirituality, he was not fenced in by that tradition. He was very much in touch with broader elements of American culture. He read widely the literature of the day. Friends outside the monastery kept him informed of the political, social, economic aspects of that culture. The multicultural dimension of his thought is well put by Lawrence S. Cunningham in the introduction to his excellent selection of Merton texts, *Thomas Merton: Spiritual Master: The Essential Writings*:

> What marked him off from other [monastic] writers...(I am thinking of his fellow Cistercian, the late Eugene Boylan, or Benedictines like Columba Marmion or Hubert Von

Zeller—all much read in their day) was his sensitivity to the modernist high culture of our time (one finds it hard to think of Columba Marmion discussing the painting of Paul Klee or the prose of André Gide) as well as his ability to communicate with those outside the world of faith (what would Eugene Boylan, say, have in common with his fellow Irishman, James Joyce?). Merton, in short, was capable of entering the larger world of cultural discourse while rooted in a tradition that gave a peculiar weight and a ring of authenticity to his words. (*Thomas Merton: Spiritual Master: The Essential Writings*, edited, with an Introduction by Lawrence S. Cunningham [Mahwah, N.J.: Paulist Press, 1992], p. 31)

Many examples could be given to illustrate Cunningham's statement. Do you know of any other monk who wrote about William Blake, James Joyce, Boris Pasternak, William Faulkner, Louis Zukofsky, Flannery O'Connor, or one who was so fascinated by French existentialism that he would write seven essays on Albert Camus? And the range of his correspondents is nothing short of amazing. Here are a few of the names: Jacques Maritain, Erich Fromm, Ernesto Cardenal, Dorothy Day, Catherine Doherty, Aldous Huxley, Bernard Haring, Henry Miller, Pope John XXIII, Pope Paul VI, Paul Tillich, Rosemary Radford Ruether, D. T. Suzuki, Rachel Carson, Louis Massignon, Mark Van Doren, and on and on.

Merton's contact with Pasternak was surely one of the highlights of his life. He considered the publication of *Dr. Zhivago* as "one of the most significant literary events of the century" (*The Literary Essays of Thomas Merton*, p. 53). He wrote to Pasternak and spoke with great admiration about the way in which he had captured the soul of Russia. "The book," he wrote, "is a world in itself...a paradise and a hell, in which the great mystical figures of Yurii and Lara stand out as Adam and Eve and though they walk in darkness walk with their hand in the hand of God" (*Courage for Truth*, p. 89). A friend in England wrote to him about Hubert Van Zeller's negative reaction to the book. (Van Zeller is one of the "spiritual" writers mentioned above by Cunningham. He was a Benedictine monk whose writings several decades ago were quite popular in Catholic circles. Though he died only in 1984, his writings are not widely read today. In fact, I do believe that they are largely forgotten.) Merton replied to his English correspondent: "[A]s for Dom Hubert Van Z.'s saying that he dropped *Zhivago* when adultery came into the picture: he is a good man and I respect him but I do not agree with everything he says. By this standard he would have to close Genesis as soon as bigamy rears its ugly head, or as soon as Abraham palms Sarah off on Pharaoh as his 'sister'" (*The Hidden Ground of Love*, p. 389). Clearly for Merton, praising the novel was not the same thing as approving of everything done by the characters in the story. Merton writes: "Zhivago of course is not a saint or a perfect hero. He is weak-willed, and his life is a confused and unsatisfactory mess. He himself knows that he has not been able to make a success of it. But the point is, he sees that in the circumstances in which he lives it is not possible to make a real success out of life—that the only honest thing is to face meaninglessness and failure with humility, and make out of it the best one can" (*Literary Essays*, p. 67).

What I am saying, in other words, is that it is my conviction that many of Merton's writings have a quality of insight into the human condition that transcends his own life and his own generation, a wisdom that sees beyond the ephemeral and the superficial to perennial human values. These are reasons why his words are able to speak to today's generation and, I expect, to generations yet to come. He belonged to his own age. He wrote in his own time in history, yet so much of what he wrote seemed to reach beyond the culture of his own time. He was supra-cultural, yet not a-historical. By that I mean he was alive to the historical circumstances in which he lived, yet not so hemmed in by cultural restraints that he could not break through them. Indeed, breaking through cultural restraints and seeing what can be is the role of the prophet. Merton was, I believe (as I said in the Introduction), a prophet who had the insight and the wisdom to see the concerns and the questions that really mattered in human life. He never claimed to have all the answers. He did have a clear insight into the issues that needed to be dealt with.

Spiritual Director for the Masses

Thomas Merton has become for many people the person whose writings they turn to for spiritual direction. This is something he did not intend and did not want. He once wrote to a correspondent that he had no disciples. He wanted no disciples. He thought he could be of no help to disciples. Become, he suggested to this correspondent, a disciple of Christ.

Yet, whether he wanted it or not, Thomas Merton, through his many writings, has directed the spiritual journey of ever so many people whose names we shall never know: people who are in communion with institutional forms of religion and, perhaps most astounding of all, people whose only link with spirituality is the monk who lived in Nelson County, Kentucky, in the Trappist monastery of Gethsemani.

Notes

[1]Wilbur H. ("Ping") Ferry, vice-president of the Center for the Study of Democratic Institutions at Santa Barbara, California, from 1954 to 1969, often supplied Merton with informational materials from the Center. He accompanied Merton in California before he left for his Asian journey.

CHAPTER THREE

The Merton Gallery: Themes to Look for in Thomas Merton's Writings

I recall some years ago being in Florence, Italy, with a tour group that was never quite able to stay on schedule. As a result, we arrived at the Uffizi Gallery just a half-hour before closing and had a whirlwind tour, during which we had no time really to look and reflect on what we were seeing. My companion on the tour remarked dryly, as we were leaving: "Well, if we see a reproduction of a painting that is in the Uffizi, we can say: 'I must have seen it, I was there.'"

It's quite frustrating to rush through an art gallery and see so many things that you don't have time to really look at any of them. In fact, in visiting a renowned gallery, it is impossible to absorb all that is there in a single visit. Better to take the time truly to look at some of the paintings with the hope of returning again (maybe even more than once) than to try to take in everything on one visit. In such a situation it is helpful to have a guide who knows the gallery and can lead you to the truly important art works that you really must get to see.

The Gallery of Merton Themes

I would like to suggest that the corpus of Merton's writings might be likened to an outstanding, highly regarded gallery. The themes that thread their way through those writings are like works of art that could be put up for viewing. I want to invite you to view some of these themes and to take the time to let your mind and heart be grasped by them. More than that, I would suggest your returning to this gallery to see them more than once. Also it will be worth your while to pay careful attention to the Merton texts which precede each theme.

Though it is a bit of temerity on my part, I am offering myself as a guide for sorting out the things in Merton's writing that are most significant and substantive, most attractive and appealing, most helpful and relevant to us and to our world. The task I have set for myself is nothing if not overwhelming. After all, Merton wrote so very, very much. Moreover, he had an incisive mind and unusual gifts of expression. It approaches rather close to arrogance for me to presume to say to you, the reader: "Here are the themes that are important in the writings of Thomas Merton." So I plead for your indulgence, though at the same time I should point out that it has been my good fortune to have spent a large amount of my time over the last fifteen years or so reading Merton and writing about him and his works. What I have written has been quite generally well received by people who are Merton scholars and by people who simply enjoy reading his works. What gives me the courage to go ahead with the daunting task I have set for myself in this chapter is the deep regard in which I hold this man and the enthusiasm I have to share with others the many spiritual, and literary, rewards that acquaintance with Merton's writings will bring.

Merton the Writer

This is, as I say, a large undertaking, for Merton was a born writer. He loved to write. He had lots of ideas on all sorts of topics and was not quite sure from one day to the next what he might write about. At one point in *Run to the Mountain*, the first volume of his journals, he asks himself: "Why do I write so much about things about which I know so little?" (p. 144). Setting aside the modesty implicit in the question (he often did know what he was talking about), I would probably answer: "Because you can't control your pen. Once it gets on a roll, you simply cannot stop it. It is, as you yourself said 'a release for the things I am full of and must try to say'" (Ibid., p. 35).

He was, therefore, by no means a one-issue person. Nor are his ideas statically set in stone. There are issues on which over time he changed his thinking quite drastically. I should make it clear, too, that, just as not every piece in an art gallery is of the highest quality, not everything Merton wrote deserves our attention as we wander through the Merton Gallery. He did his share of poor writing, as one might expect of someone who wrote as much (and often as hurriedly) as he did. I want to insist on this, because I would not want to turn Merton into an oracle whose every word must be accepted as gospel-truth.

His writing can at times be frivolous, conceited, arrogant, dogmatic, overly erudite. His penchant for superlatives is frequently evident. But there is so much that is good, wise, thought-provoking, insightful, profound, witty, clever: so much that our world needs to hear. There are splendid passages of reflection that touch deeply into the human soul, and there are passages brimming over with fun and humor when he plays with ideas and words and sentences and shows a sharp eye for the foibles in human nature, including his own.

I am eager, therefore, to share his best with you. Obviously when I say "his best," that will mean what I consider his best. For, as Naomi Burton Stone, Merton's literary agent and close friend, has written: "Each one of us knows a different Thomas Merton." Though she was speaking of those who knew him personally, what she wrote is also true of those whose only acquaintance with him has been through his writings. Some will be drawn to the room in the gallery marked "contemplation" and will find his best writing there. Others will look for the best in the social criticism or the literary criticism section or the poetry. At times the rooms will overlap with one another: For instance, thoughts on solitude will be close to the room marked "contemplation." A growing number of people, while not ignoring the other rooms, will seek out the one labeled "the East." In short, his thoughts and reflections appeal to many different people who have different interests and who come to the gallery for quite a number of different reasons.

Since a variety of interests draw people to different rooms in the Merton Gallery, it might be helpful, in approaching a study of what to look for in those various rooms, to clarify the different ways in which people think of Merton. In much of the writing that has been done about him a number of different images, not all compatible with one another, have emerged.

The "multiple images" of Thomas Merton arise, I believe, out of three different *visions* people have of Gethsemani's most famous monk. These three visions are perhaps best understood in terms of the different views people have taken about Merton's subsequent relationship to the book whose thoughts and reflections have a special place in the Merton Gallery, the book that must be called his greatest, or at least his most influential, *The Seven Storey Mountain*.

The Different Ways People View Thomas Merton

‿A. Faithful to the Vision of The Seven Storey Mountain‿

The first of these three visions belongs to those whose Merton has remained, quite statically, faithful to the insights of *The Seven Storey Mountain*. For them Merton is still the quiet, ascetic monk, with downcast eyes and an otherworldly visage who spoke eloquently of prayer and called people to avoid the world and its allurements as much as possible. Those who cling to this vision of Thomas Merton are the ones who ask for relics of him and wonder when he will be canonized. No reputable Merton scholar would even think of adopting this view today.

～B. Betraying the Vision of The Seven Storey Mountain ～

The second attitude toward Thomas Merton sees him as the man who *betrayed* the vision of *The Seven Storey Mountain*. Those who view him this way may, in turn, be divided into two groups. First, there are those who *applaud* him for that betrayal. In this category are people who see Merton as a man of frustration and burnt-out faith, who abandoned Christianity and monasticism and whose full apostasy never became known because he died accidentally before he was able to make public the decision to give up all that *The Seven Storey Mountain* had stood for.

The most scholarly representation of this image of Merton is a book written by Dr. David Cooper. Entitled *Thomas Merton's Art of Denial: The Evolution of a Radical Humanist*, Cooper's book may well be the most challenging book yet to have been written about Thomas Merton. Elegant in its prose style, carefully thought out and well organized in structure, it is iconoclastic in its thesis. Cooper's Merton is a one-time monk who grew up into a "post-Christian secular humanist." Unable to achieve the heights of "infused" contemplation, he came to accept the fact that he had "failed as a mystic," not for lack of trying, but because he finally saw that the monastic goal was an unrealizable ideal. But this admission of failure was not loss but gain. It freed him from the shackles of an outmoded worldview, enabled him to integrate his humanness, and opened him once again to the world he had abandoned and to the responsibilities he was now ready to assume for that world. Merton became a modern man. The author, who for twenty years had let himself be satisfied with writing inspirational and devotional works, began to produce incisive social and literary criticism. Thomas Merton, the monk, the solitary, became—in the 1960's—the radical humanist, for whom withdrawal gave place to engagement, separation to involvement.

David Cooper is a good friend of mine, but—as he knows—I completely reject his thesis. His book is very well written, but in my opinion its argument ignores many important texts that do not support his thesis. Moreover, he fails to realize that, when Merton writes that he is a failure as a mystic, Merton is using the *lingua franca* of mystical writers. No mystic ever says: "I am a mystic." He or she might well say: "I'm no mystic at all. I am a sinner." This is not a false humility, but a deep realization of the huge gulf between himself or herself and God.

There is, on the other hand, a second group of people who feel that Merton betrayed the vision of *The Seven Storey Mountain*, but who are *appalled* at what eventually happened to this monk, who in *The Seven Storey Mountain* gave such marvelous promise of a holy and edifying future. The most vocal expression of this attitude toward Merton has appeared on a sadly biased video cassette made by Alice von Hildebrand (who continually reminds her hearers that she was the wife of the late Dietrich von Hildebrand, a well-known Catholic writer of the pre-Vatican II era, who found much of the Vatican II reform problematic). This cassette (a "Keep the Faith" production) carried the ominous title: *The Tragedy of Thomas Merton*. A bitter attack, delivered by a stern-faced Mrs. von Hildebrand, its intent is to warn Christians against the dangers into which this "fallen" monk could lead them. Its substance is the accusation that Merton returned to the temptations of his youth which seemingly he had abandoned when he became a monk. The "temptations" were to a dabbling in (1) psychoanalysis, (2) Eastern religions and (3) communism. An example of the crudity of her picture of Merton is the conviction she expresses that his involvement in the antiwar issue and his condemnation of the war in Viet Nam are instances of his move to the far left and, for her, this meant communism. ✒

⌁⌁C. *Going Beyond* The Seven Storey Mountain ⌁⌁

There is yet a third category of Merton readers, followers and scholars, namely, those who believe that Merton has *gone far beyond The Seven Storey Mountain*. They recognize that for all its charismatic appeal (and that appeal, amazingly, continues to be experienced by new Merton readers), *The Seven Storey Mountain* has many weaknesses: the narrowness of its theology, the smug sense of belonging to the "true" Church, the frequent "put-downs" of other Christian Churches, the brushing aside of Eastern religions as worthless, the sharp separation of the supernatural from the natural, the homiletic tone that interlaces the text with sermons and *fervorinos*, not unlike those Catholics were hearing from the pulpit on Sunday. If *The Seven Storey Mountain* continues to appeal to a whole new generation of readers (as surely it does), this is not because of, but in spite of, its theological stance. For today's readers the magnanimity of the writer somehow transcends the narrowness of his theology.

And those readers, old or new, who continue to read what Merton wrote in the two decades following the publication of *The Seven Storey Mountain* are quite ready to excuse the rigidity and even prejudice that surface in *The Seven Storey Mountain*, because they have come to realize how far beyond *The Seven Storey Mountain* Merton had gone. Writing in 1966, he said:

> [D]ue to a book I wrote thirty years ago, I have myself become a sort of stereotype of the world-denying contemplative—the man who spurned New York, spat on Chicago, and tromped on Louisville, heading for the woods with Thoreau in one pocket, John of the Cross in another, and holding the Bible open at the Apocalypse. This personal stereotype is probably my own fault, and it is something I have to try to demolish on occasion. (*Contemplation in a World of Action*, pp. 143-144)

He continues (and, remember, he is writing in 1966, two years before his death):

> I want to make clear that I speak not as the author of *The Seven Storey Mountain*, which seemingly a lot of people have read, but as the author of more recent essays and poems which apparently very few people have read. This is

not the official voice of Trappist silence, the monk with his hood up and his back to the camera, brooding over the waters of an artificial lake. This is not the petulant and uncanonizable modern Jerome who never got over the fact that he could give up beer. (I drink beer whenever I can lay my hands on any. I love beer, and, by that very fact, the world.)

Having said who it is who is not speaking, he goes on to identify who he now is.

This is simply the voice of a self-questioning human person who, like all his brothers [and sisters], struggles to cope with turbulent, mysterious, demanding, exciting, frustrating, confused existence in which almost nothing is really predictable, in which most definitions...and justifications become incredible even before they are uttered, in which people suffer together and are sometimes utterly beautiful, at other times impossibly pathetic. In which there is much that is frightening, in which almost everything public is patently phony, and in which there is at the same time an immense ground of personal authenticity that is right there and so obvious that no one can talk about it and most cannot even believe that it is there.

The conclusion he draws situates him squarely in the contemporary world:

I am...a man in the modern world.... Where am I going to look for the world first of all if not in myself?

...As long as I imagine that the world is something to be "escaped" in a monastery—that wearing a special costume and following a quaint observance takes me "out of this world," I am dedicating my life to an illusion.

From what I have quoted, it should be clear that Merton had indeed undergone considerable change in his thinking on many subjects and in the way he saw his monastic vocation. In May 1967 he completed *Cables to the Ace*. In the prologue to this long poem (really an anti-poem, employing irony, experiment, parody, macabre fantasy, counterpoint of sense and nonsense), he indicates a change in his intellectual geography, in his approach to life and in the audience he seeks to reach. The poet, he says, speaking of himself, "has changed his address and his poetics are on vacation. He is not roaring in the old tunnel." It is no longer in any tunnel that he is roaring: More and more it is in the wide open spaces of a world he has rediscovered for what it is in all its sinfulness and all its grandeur. There is a whole new room in the gallery.

Indeed, even in the same room in the gallery, we shall be seeing his thoughts and reflections differing from one another, simply because Merton was continually growing and was never one to feel that he had said the last word on any subject. He was always interested in new ideas, new visions, new insights. Especially in his later years, he was a complex figure who cannot be described in one single way. He is a Merton of many images, of many paradoxes. I want almost to say: a Merton of many contradictions. In October 1968, when in Alaska, he gave a series of talks at the convent of the Precious Blood Sisters. In the course of one of these talks, he discusses an article by Martin Buber, in which Buber speaks of people who have "complex, self-contradictory temperaments." In a very jovial manner, he confesses to the sisters that he could tell them a good deal about that kind of temperament, because (he says) it is "a perfect description of me."

Inconsistency and Stability

I believe that Merton was not being facetious: He was giving a rather apt description of himself. His temperament was, indeed, "complex and self-contradictory," though I would want to soften a bit the notion of "self-contradictory" and perhaps have it mean: "one who had the capability of combining in himself ideas, attitudes, convictions that seem to be incompatible with one another." He had a mind and a heart big enough to contain the apparently irreconcilable, without having them explode within him. On the contrary, it was in striving to bring together what often seemed to be in conflict that he eventually was able to move in the direction of true simplicity and personal integration in his life. To what extent he achieved this simplicity and that integration is a question that is still very much on the table. ❧

My approach to an answer would be to suggest that the fundamental paradox of Thomas Merton can be expressed in two words: *inconsistency* and *stability*. It is my conviction that in his life and in his writings, he managed to combine both of these in a creative tension that, in the end, brought a large measure of unity and integration into his life.

I need to clarify, in the first place, what I mean by "inconsistency." I would like to contrast it with the word "consistent," taken in its fundamental etymological meaning. I take "consistent" to mean something like: "standing firmly in one place, knowing why one is there and what one must do." If one accepts this meaning of "consistent," then Merton in his later years can hardly be described as "consistent." The Merton of the 1960's (and even the late 1950's) scarcely ever stayed in one place—intellectually, creatively, spiritually. In fact, he was all over the lot. His enthusiasms carried him in all sorts of directions. He writes on a wide variety of subjects. While he does not actually master any of them (because he moved so often from one to another), he had the wonderful talent of being able to go to the heart of a subject, articulate it with unusual clarity and then go on to something else. In his later years one is never quite sure where he is going to be, and what is going to be his concern of the moment. He opens doors for others (in the imaginary gallery we are thinking about) to rooms that he hardly ever lingers in, because he is too occupied in searching out other doors.

This is why I wrote in my biography of Merton, *Silent Lamp*, that "though his best-seller autobiography was 439 pages long, he was not, generally speaking, at his best in sustained writing."

> The literary genre in which he tended to excel...was the polished essay or the well-crafted letter.... He writes

knowledgeably about...the Shakers, Zen, the medieval mystics...Chinese philosophy, the Crusades, and many more subjects.... From the summer of 1961 to the spring of 1962, his writing is heavily concentrated on the issue of war and peace.... In the years that followed, while not completely dropping that issue, his concerns tended to move in other directions. The point is that what he was doing at the moment seemed to be the most important thing in the world for him; yet he is neither slow nor loath to move into totally other areas. (*Silent Lamp*, p. 20)

In his concern to make a point, he often exaggerates. In his desire to respect the sensibilities of others, he often bends over backwards to make his position compatible with theirs. Of this latter tendency there is perhaps no better example than his extraordinary correspondence with Rosemary Radford Ruether (which perhaps deserves a room all its own in the gallery). Merton seemed quite fascinated with being, even if only by mail, in the company of "a woman theologian." He very much wanted to agree with what she said. Thus, when she caustically questions the whole meaning of the monastic life, he is eager to side with her. So he tells her that, as a hermit, he is really a "non-monk," just a kind of "tramp" living in the woods. (See *The Hidden Ground of Love*, pp. 497-516.)

Yet—note the inconsistency—during the quite brief period of their rather fiery correspondence, he was at the same time writing articles and offering advice to monastic groups about how the monastic life needed to be and could be renewed in our day. Moreover, when Ruether suggested that he give up the pretense he was living by, leave the monastery and come out into the world where he could engage in battle with the "real demons," he has no doubt what his answer must be. Though his presence there may seem useless in her eyes, he was convinced that he was where God wanted him to be: in the woods—living his hermit existence.

Rootedness

This conviction that in the midst of much change, turmoil and uncertainty he was yet where God willed him to be is the essential *stability* that gives a *rootedness* to his life and its seeming inconsistencies. To have stability is somewhat like being in a circle that always has a center; and if one is deeply rooted in that center, he or she can move to any point on the circumference of that circle without losing balance. Moreover, one can go back to that center from the perplexities of the circumference, not always or necessarily to find solutions to those perplexities, but to find at the very least that one is moving in the right direction and grappling with the issues that really matter. If you will, one can afford to be "inconsistent," if one is deeply enough rooted in a center. In his journal, *A Vow of Conversation*, Merton wrote: "My ideas are always changing, always moving around one center, and I am always seeing that center from somewhere else. Hence I will always be accused of inconsistency. But I will no longer be there to hear the accusation" (p. 19).

I strongly believe that Merton had such a center and that center, I would maintain, was his monastic vocation. During his life in the monastery Merton exercised many roles: writer, novice-master, spiritual director, social activist, nonviolent revolutionist—but he did all as a monk. It is my conviction that it is his monastic vocation that unifies his life and offers a focus for looking at the "many images" that the facts of his life and the directions of his thought bring to light.

Perhaps at this point I might ask those who have read *The Seven Storey Mountain* and a bit beyond, which of these three visions best expresses your present feeling about Merton and the way you approach his writings? Or, if you are unacquainted with Merton, which "Merton" would you prefer to hear about? I quite readily make clear my own bias when I suggest that the only approach that is ultimately fruitful (and fair to him) is the third, namely, the approach that sees Merton as someone, who, while rising to fame because of *The Seven Storey Mountain*, continued to evolve his

thinking and eventually went far beyond the positions he
had taken in that great modern classic.

Eight Themes

I have chosen eight themes which I believe are important in
understanding Merton and his writings. Two ways of
presenting these themes suggest themselves. I could simply
pile up quotations from Merton that relate to each of them. To
some degree I have done this by prefixing quotations from
his writings to each theme. A second approach—the one I
mainly choose to follow—is to present these themes as I have
come to understand them, as they have come to have
meaning for me. I realize that in doing so I run the risk of
making Merton say what I want him to say. Readers may find
themselves at times asking: "Is this Merton or Shannon?" I
can only respond to such a question: "This is Shannon
interpreting Merton, trying to unpack the depth of meaning
that can be discovered in these themes." If I sometimes refer
to personal experiences (as occasionally I shall), it is because
they have helped me to do some of that "unpacking."

～～～ 1. Interiority: Speaking Out for the Inside ～～～

*I break through the superficial exterior appearances that form my
routine vision of the world and my own self, and I find myself in
the presence of hidden majesty.* (New Seeds of Contemplation,
p. 41)

*The only true joy on earth is to escape from the prison of our own
false self and enter by love into union with the Life Who dwells
and sings within the essence of every creature and in the core of
our own souls. (Ibid., p. 25)*

*Our real journey in life is interior: it is a matter of growth,
deepening, and an ever greater surrender to the creative action
of love and grace in our hearts.* (The Road to Joy, p. 118)

I have spoken about the centrality of Merton's monastic

vocation. Does this mean that only monks can enter appreciatively into the gallery of Merton themes? I think not. For, though Merton wrote as a monk, he did not write simply (I am tempted to say, even primarily) for monks. His intended readership was just people; or perhaps I should say, people who realize all too clearly that they are living on the surface of life and instinctively feel that there is more to life than what they are presently experiencing. In a letter to John Hunt, senior editor of *The Saturday Evening Post*, he offers us an indication of the kind of readers to whom he hoped his writings would appeal.

In December 1966 Hunt had extended him an invitation to write a guest article for the magazine's opinion column called "Speaking Out." Knowing Merton to be something of a famous monk, he understandably asked him to write about the monastic life.

Merton saw in this invitation an opportunity to say things to the readers of *The Saturday Evening Post* that in his mind were much more important than anything he could say about monasteries and the monastic life. Such information they could look up in a good encyclopedia. He wanted to tell people about the deeper realities of life which they could discover within themselves, if only they looked. He wanted them to understand that human life has an interior dimension. At the same time, he wanted to warn them that life's circumstances can easily prevent them from ever reaching this dimension of life. He knew all too well that a person can live almost entirely on the outside of life without ever suspecting the depths of reality that are within. He suggested to Hunt, therefore, that he write an article with the title "Speaking Out *for the Inside*."

But Hunt knew what he wanted from this monk and apparently was unimpressed by the alternative Merton had proposed. Merton's proposal was rejected. He made no appearance in the pages of *The Saturday Evening Post*.

We might wish that Hunt had accepted Merton's suggestions for an article. It would be good to know what he would say "speaking out for the inside." Fortunately, we are not left entirely in the dark, as Merton did manage in his letter to Hunt to give some idea of what he would include in the article he planned to write.

The intent of the article he proposed was to help people come to know that "inside" of themselves that he wanted to "speak out for." He hoped to make people aware of the inner depths of their being. There is much more to life than meets the eye. There is a world of reality below and above (indeed all around) our ordinary daily experience. It is that world alone that ultimately is real. Merton writes of "the overwhelming and almost totally neglected importance of exploring this spiritual unconscious of man. There is no real love of life unless it is oriented to the discovery of one's true, spiritual self, beyond and above the level of mere empirical individuality, with its superficial enjoyments and fears" (*Faith and Violence*, p. 112). Yet, so many people are oblivious of this world of interiority. For it is effectively blocked out by a life that concentrates on externals. People are so often taken up with things outside themselves that they have no time for what is "inside." Hence they lack an inner center from which they can live their lives. Without that center they inevitably find themselves living in division and fragmentation, as they experience themselves being pulled in many different and often opposing directions.

A life of this sort is one of inner poverty. For those who live this way never, or hardly ever, have the time to discover their own identity. For our identity is to be found not in what we *do*, but in who we *are*. And who we are cannot be discovered in our activities, worthwhile and praiseworthy though they may be, but in our *being*, which can only be experienced in that "inside" for which Merton wanted to "speak out."

How mightily our lives would be changed if we became aware of life's other, deeper dimensions. Lacking that awareness, we are in a situation not unlike that of the people of Europe before the New World was discovered. Knowing only Europe, they were totally unaware that a whole other world, holding out new and exciting adventures, was there waiting to be discovered. When finally they came to know of its existence, their history was irrevocably changed. In a similar way, people who know only the externals of human living are cut off from a realm of their own reality that could offer them new and exciting experiences far surpassing the kind of living that is possible at the level of just the superficial.

What we all need, Merton declares, is an *inner* freedom and an *inner* vision. We move toward that freedom and vision, he maintains, only when we relate ourselves to something within us that we *don't really know*.

At first hearing, you may want to say: That doesn't sound very helpful. What in the world does he mean by "something within us" that "we don't know" and yet have to "relate ourselves to"? Does he mean the "psychological unconscious"? No, he is very emphatic that this is not what he is talking about. That "something" we don't know, yet have to relate to, is, he suggests, the spiritual unconscious, what Paul Tillich, in *The Courage to Be*, called the ground of being (and I may add, what Merton himself called "The Hidden Ground of Love."[1] Traditionally, he says, that "something" we are related to is called God. But, Merton is careful to warn us not to try to identify that "something" with ideas and images of God that we may have in our heads. For ideas and images are unable to comprehend the reality of God. (We shall talk more about this later.)

Merton is really writing about a contemplative way of relating to God (a way that goes beyond ideas and images), rather than a devotional way. Devotional spirituality concerns itself chiefly with images of God (and that is fine, but of necessity it has its limitations). Contemplative spirituality goes beyond images and ideas, which can only partially represent God, to the very Reality of God, the Reality of the divine Self. It is only in relating to this divine Reality that we achieve a measure of inner freedom and inner vision.

As Merton puts it in the letter to Hunt: "The real inner life and freedom of man begin when this inner dimension opens up and man lives in communion with the unknown within him." But that is not all. He goes on to say: "On the basis of this he can also be in communion with the same unknown in others" (*Witness to Freedom*, pp. 329-330). That is the core of the Christian experience: communion with the unknown within us and, at the same time, communion with that same unknown in others.

He concluded his letter to the editor of *The Saturday Evening Post* by saying: "This is rather tough and will demand a lot from your readers.... My suggestion is: frankly admit the toughness and unpalatableness of the subject and treat it as it is. Some may be hit hard, most will remain indifferent."

Such a description of what he intended to say was hardly calculated to "sell" his idea to the editor. I know editors well enough to realize that they are not interested in material that their readers would find "tough and unpalatable," nor do they care about stuff that most readers would "remain indifferent" to. In describing his proposed article the way he did, Merton was clearly writing his own rejection slip. And in his enthusiasm for what he wanted to say, he seemed to have no idea that he was doing so. ✽

A Mistake on Merton's Part?

I pause a moment to ask you to reflect on these questions: Was this a blunder on Merton's part? Should he have taken the opportunity to write about monasticism? Perhaps he should have. After all, interiority is what the monastic life is all about. Why did he not write about monasticism and, in that context, say all the things he wanted to say to his readers about inner freedom and inner vision? I believe the reason he did not choose this approach was his conviction that this delving into one's depths and being in touch with the truly Real within us was a task for everyone, not just for monks. By 1966 Merton was too deeply aware of the needs of people outside the monastery to risk having readers think that he believed otherwise. *Discovering one's inner depths and finding*

God there is not just a monastic endeavor; it is a human one. It is central to the human "thirst for authentic existence" of which the philosopher Martin Heidegger speaks. Only God can satisfy that thirst.

In his writings on spirituality Merton is constantly pointing to the existence of this marvelous interior life in all of us. When we miss it, we miss most of what is truly real in us and around us. To speak of the divine presence as the heart and center of that interior life in us is simply to put into other words a general truth which is at the core of all true Christian spirituality, namely, "that God is everywhere." When we begin to experience God in the depths of our own being, then this wondrous truth "God is everywhere," ceases to be merely an article of faith we learned in a religion class. It becomes, instead, a reality of personal experience: what Merton calls a "communion with the Unknown" within us.

A large room, then, in the Merton Gallery would have to be called "Interiority." Indeed, this notion is so central to his thinking that it might give its name to the whole gallery.

2. Prayer: The Journey Toward Interiority— Contemplative Spirituality

Contemplation reaches out to the knowledge and even to the experience of the transcendent and inexpressible God.... [It is a] vivid awareness of infinite Being at the roots of our own limited being. (New Seeds of Contemplation, pp. 2, 3)

Contemplation is no pain-killer.... It is a terrible breaking and burning of idols, a purification of the sanctuary, so that no graven thing may occupy the place that God has commanded to be left empty: the center, the existential altar which simply "is." (Ibid., p. 13)

Since God cannot be imagined, anything our imagination tells us about Him is ultimately misleading and therefore we cannot know Him as He really is unless we pass beyond everything that can be imagined and enter into an obscurity without images and without the likeness of any created thing. (Ibid., p. 131)

Faith is not just conformity [to formulas of doctrine], it is life. It embraces all the realms of life, penetrating into the most mysterious and inaccessible depths not only of our own unknown spiritual being but even of God's own hidden essence and love. (Ibid., p. 137)

Many times I find myself wishing that we had a concordance of Merton's writings. A concordance would make it easy to locate Merton texts we remember reading, but can't recall where we read them. It would help us also to find the many ways in which he used a particular term. It would enable us to clarify his understanding of a particular topic by putting together the things he wrote on that topic. I hope someday this project will come to fruition. Anybody out there who would like to help?

It would be interesting to guess which topic would have the most entries in such a concordance. I would be willing to bet that "contemplation" would be near the top or at the top. In one of his early books of poetry there is a poem based on Psalm 137. The psalmist, writing in exile, vows the depth of his commitment to the holy city of Jerusalem. Plaintively, he cries out: "Let my tongue cling to the roof of my mouth, if I do not remember you, ...Jerusalem...." In his poem Merton pictures himself as an exile seeking the land of promise and makes the vow:

May my bones burn and ravens eat my flesh,
    If I forget thee, contemplation.

Though this poem was written early in his monastic life (1949), I believe it can be said that he remained faithful to its commitment to the very end. And that commitment involved not only making his own life contemplative but helping others to do the same.

Contemplation: The Impossible Dream?

As I write this, I wonder when you, the reader, first heard about contemplation? Was it in connection with certain extraordinary people (John of the Cross, Teresa of Avila and such like) who achieved a life of contemplation? If this was the case, did your reading about them help you to see contemplation as a viable experience for yourself? Or was it something to admire in these unusual people, but hardly something that could find a place in your own life? I ask these questions because I believe that many people in the not-too-distant past thought of contemplation as an elitist experience given only to a few and not even to be thought of by the rest of us. And many today, I believe, still think that way. In fact, I quite readily admit that that was my thinking for all too long a time in my life. What changed my attitude and encouraged me to think that contemplation was a possibility for me was my reading Merton and studying his writings.

Contemplation: Dangerous Involvement?

In fact, I can remember the first talk I gave inviting people to look to contemplation as the ordinary flowering of the baptismal vocation. It was some time in the early 1970's. I was then a member of the liturgical commission of our diocese and was invited to address the commission at its annual day of retreat. It was the time in my life when I was beginning to study Merton's writings in earnest, especially what he had to say about contemplation. I decided to throw discretion to the wind and talk about "The Contemplative Dimensions of the Sacraments." My talk was followed by a rather heated discussion. One of the commission members was quite uneasy about what I had said. "My concern," he told us, "is that contemplation is a dangerous thing to get involved in. It means delving into areas of our lives that are deep and ambiguous and confusing. Encouraging people to be contemplatives could easily lead them astray."

I was quite willing to admit that talking about contemplation (at least at that time) was a bit daring and getting involved in it (at practically any time) could easily be dangerous. It's dangerous because it leads me into unexplored areas of my person. It is dangerous because it puts me into contact with my contingency, my utter dependence, my nothingness. Contemplation is, to quote Merton: "[a]n awareness of our contingent reality as received, as a present from God, as a free gift of love" (*New Seeds of Contemplation*, p. 3). My ego gets pushed out of the central place in my life, for that place belongs only to God. In Merton's words: "The only true joy on earth is to escape from the prison of our own self-hood...and enter by love into union with the Life Who dwells and sings within the essence of every creature and in the core of our own souls" (*Seeds of Contemplation*, p. 22).

More than all this, contemplation undoes my perception of God. I come to realize that I do not know who God is at all. Up to then I had thought that my language was adequate to deal with God. But in contemplation I am in the presence of a Reality I do not understand, I am Jacob struggling through the night and demanding of his "Adversary": "What is your name?" and receiving no answer. I am like Zachary in the temple, struck dumb by what he experienced. The words I used to use so glibly now stick in my throat. I thought I knew how to say: "God." Now I am reduced to silence. No matter what I say about God it is so far from the divine Reality that I am forced to unsay it. I find myself blinded by the dazzling light of a Reality I thought I knew.

Fallen Idols Along the Contemplative Way

All along the contemplative way lie fallen images of the false gods that I had created or my culture or my religion had created for me and that now I have to give up, for they are no more than idols. A few examples: the god who is "up there," not "here"; the god who is an object or a being (even supreme being) among other beings; the god with whom I carry on friendly, cozy conversations; the god made in the image of my own prejudices (who is probably white, male and American); the god who rewards and punishes; the god who is so obviously male and paternalistic. Contemplation, Merton says, "is a terrible breaking and burning of idols, a purification of the sanctuary, so that no graven thing may occupy the place that God has commanded to be left empty: the center, the existential altar which simply 'is.' In the end the contemplative suffers the anguish of realizing that he *no longer knows what God is*" (*New Seeds of Contemplation*, p. 13).

When contemplation begins to "take hold" in our lives, we are conscious, without fully understanding it, that we are *in* this God whom we can no longer name and that this God is in us. Distinct from God, we are yet not separate from God. We feel scorched by the terrifying immediacy of the presence of One whom we had thought we could keep at a safe and comfortable distance. We find that this God cannot be kept in a safe or predetermined place: This God is everywhere.

Getting back to my talk to the diocesan liturgical commission, I readily confess I would not have given that talk (in fact would not even have thought of giving it), were it not for Thomas Merton. He was writing a chunk of American history when he wrote in *The Seven Storey Mountain*: "America is discovering the contemplative life" (p. 414). And for many (myself included) he was the spiritual master who led the way to that discovery. As I have said on many occasions, Thomas Merton made "contemplation" a household word.

Teach Contemplation? No Way!

This is not to say that he was a teacher of contemplation. As he himself put it, it is as impossible to attempt to teach people "how to be a contemplative," as it would be to teach them "how to be an angel." (See *New Seeds of Contemplation*, p. x.) For contemplation is an awakening to a whole new level of reality, which cannot even be clearly explained. "It can only be hinted at, suggested, pointed to, symbolized" (Ibid., p. 6). He did believe, however, that an aptitude for contemplation can be awakened in people. But this is possible only if they have already had good human experiences. Only those who have learned to *see* with their own eyes, *hear* with their own ears, *taste* with their own tongues and *experience* with their whole being are apt candidates for the contemplative life. Television addicts, people whose lives continually need external stimulation, who have never opened themselves to their own inner truth, live lives so low in authenticity that a contemplative life would simply be out of their reach. They need to have opportunities for normal wholesome human experiences before it makes any sense even to talk to them about contemplation. And let us face the fact that the culture we live in, with its emphasis on the external and the superficial, its penchant for pleasure and ease, its production-driven mentality, its tendency to emphasize rights over responsibilities, does not provide good soil in which the good seed of contemplation can grow and develop.

We Are All Contemplatives!

Yet that seed is really present in all of us. There is a sense in which it can be said that we are all contemplatives, because whether we know it or not we are *in God*. This interiority and depth are present in all of us and can be reached by those who are willing to submit to the discipline that a contemplative way of life demands. While this discipline may require a change in behavior, its principal aim is to achieve a transformation of consciousness whereby we view reality differently. We discover the true God at the very center of our being and ourselves as nothing apart from God. With this discovery a new life dawns. We are liberated from selfishness. The ego-self (which in reality is a false self) is discarded like "an old snake skin" (to use Merton's words) and we come to recognize our true self which all the while had been hidden in God. The true self is not a separate or isolated reality, but one with everyone and everything in God. Thus we find not only our own identity, but also our inextricable link with all our sisters and brothers in God. This is the contemplative vision. It begets compassion and nonviolent love. (More about this later.)

Contemplation: Awakening to the Real in All Reality

This is why Merton tells us over and over that contemplation is a state of heightened consciousness. "Contemplation," he writes, "is the highest expression of man's intellectual and spiritual life. It is that life itself, fully awake, fully active, fully aware that it is alive" (*New Seeds of Contemplation*, p. 1). One is reminded of Evelyn Underhill's words: "Only the mystic can be called a whole man, since in others half the powers of the self always sleep" (*Mysticism*, p. 63).

Contemplation, Merton tells us, is "an awakening to the Real in all that is real" (*New Seeds of Contemplation*, p. 3). The word "real" is an important word in the Merton vocabulary. If you look to the *Oxford English Dictionary*, you will find "real" described as applying "to whatever is regarded as having an existence in fact and not merely in appearance, thought or language or as having an absolute, a necessary, in contrast to a merely contingent, existence." Now that definition of "real" may not make you jump up and down with joy. Not many definitions do! But this OED statement makes an important distinction. The word "real" has two meanings. It may mean that which exists in fact, but contingently. To exist contingently indicates dependence: It means existing not on one's own, but derivatively. It means deriving one's existence from another. The second meaning of "real" designates that which not only exists in fact, but exists absolutely and necessarily. What exists absolutely and necessarily exists in its own right, totally independent of anything or anyone else. Since the contingently "real" depends on the absolutely "Real," to see the first aright one must see the second. In other words, you do not see the "contingently real" as it truly is, until you see it in the absolutely "Real." When you achieve this vision, you have achieved the contemplative vision. This is the meaning of Merton's words which I quoted at the beginning of this paragraph: "Contemplation is an awakening to the [absolutely] Real in all that is [contingently] real." To be unaware of God at the heart of all reality, as the Source and Sustainer of all that is, is to fail to see reality as it is. It is to pretend that the contingently real can exist without the absolutely Real. It is going through life half-awake, or even worse, it is to live a contradiction.

On January 15, 1966, Merton responds to a correspondent who was involved in helping people make career changes, and who asks Merton if he has any advice for such people. Merton replies that, whatever the changes may be that we make in life, "[w]e should decide not in view of better pay, higher rank, 'getting ahead,' but in view of becoming *more real*, entering more authentically into direct contact with life" (*Witness to Freedom*, p. 255). Direct contact with life means recognizing the derivative existence of everything that is and awakening to the presence of God, from whom all reality derives. It is to awaken to the contemplative dimension of reality. It is the discovery of God within us.

Two Ways of Prayer

In 1961 Thomas Merton put together a fifty-three-page collection of prayers for the novices at Gethsemani. It includes selections from the Scriptures, the Fathers of the Church, the Cistercian Fathers of the thirteenth century, the English mystics and others. The most interesting part of the book for me is the one-page introduction that Merton himself wrote. In this introduction, he speaks of two kinds of prayer: "Prayer is not only the 'lifting up of the mind and heart to God,' but also the response to God within us, the discovery of God within us." The first type of prayer is probably the one we are most accustomed to: lifting the mind and heart to God, generally with words. This is often called vocal prayer, prayer in which we use words to praise, thank and petition God as well as to express our repentance. The second type of prayer to which Merton refers, "response to God within, the discovery of God within us," is a way of prayer that is less familiar to most people. This is the prayer of silence, when we try simply to *be* in the presence of God, without words, thoughts, ideas. It is sometimes called "centering prayer" or "prayer of the heart" or "prayer of awareness."

Contemplation as the Highest Degree of Awareness of God

There are various degrees of awareness of God's presence in our lives or of our "discovery of God within us." The highest degree is what we call contemplative prayer. Contemplative prayer, which is so total an awareness of God that nothing can distract us from the divine presence, is not something we can earn. It is not something we do. It is always God's special gift, given not on demand, but when and as often as God wills it. Yet our God is a generous God who does not withhold gifts when we are ready for them. Merton writes in that page of introduction to the Selections of Prayer:

> Prayer is an expression of our complete dependence on a hidden and mysterious God. It is therefore nourished by humility.... We should never seek to reach some supposed "summit of prayer" out of spiritual ambition. We should seek to enter deep into the life of prayer, not in order that we may glory in it as an "achievement," but because in this way we can come close to the Lord Who seeks to do us good, Who seeks to give us His mercy, and to surround us with His love. To love prayer is, then, to love our own poverty and His mercy.

What a great sentence that: To love prayer is to love our own poverty and God's mercy!

Daily Perseverance

If we are to prepare ourselves for this total awareness of God's presence which is contemplation, we need to spend time in silence and quiet, simply being in God's presence. This needs to be a daily practice. Perseverance is the key. Humility is the disposition: a willingness to admit how distracted we so often are, yet the determination to be more attentive, realizing that God wills our attentiveness so much more than we do or ever could.

Perseverance will inevitably effect changes in the way we live our lives. Experiencing our oneness with God brings the realization that what is true of us is true of all our sisters and brothers: They too are one with God. This makes it possible for us to experience our oneness with them and indeed with all that is. We are more alert to treat people with love and concern, because we experience that oneness. ❧

Methods of Prayer?

After several years as novice master, Merton was pleased with the way his novices were "progressing" in prayer. He was not overly directive regarding their prayer-life. On the contrary, writing in September 1964, he said to one of his correspondents (and what he says is a helpful word for us too):

> I must say that there is a good proportion of contemplative prayer in the novitiate. I don't use special methods. I try to make them love the freedom and peace of being with God alone in faith and simplicity, to abolish all divisiveness and diminish all useless strain and concentration on one's own efforts.... (*The Hidden Ground of Love*, p. 368)

Etta Gullick, a correspondent living in England, once challenged Merton to write an article on "Progress in Prayer." He was not too enthusiastic about doing the article. He wrote to her: "In the long run I think progress in prayer comes from the Cross and humiliation and whatever makes us really experience our total poverty and nothingness, and also gets our minds off ourselves" (Ibid., p. 376).

This is a good text on which to close our reflection on contemplation. "Getting our minds off ourselves" is key. As Merton wrote in *The Sign of Jonas*: "If we would find God in the depths of our souls we have to leave everybody else outside, including ourselves" (p. 48). Even more emphatically in an earlier text in that journal, he puts it very simply: "[T]he important thing is not to live for contemplation, but to live for God" (p. 30).

The "contemplative" room in the Merton Gallery is easily entered, as one leaves the room marked "Interiority." And inevitably these two rooms are very close to the one marked "God."

So much depends on our idea of God! Yet no idea of Him,
however pure and perfect, is adequate to express Him as He really
is. Our idea of God tells us more about ourselves than about
Him. (New Seeds of Contemplation, *p. 15*)

[O]ur knowledge of [God] is no longer merely as though it were
the knowledge of an "object"! (Who could bear such a thing: and
yet religious people do it: just as if the world contained here a
chair, there a house, there a hill, and then again God. As if the
identity of all were not hidden in Him Who has no name.) (The
Road to Joy, *p. 26*)

We can find ourself engulfed in such happiness that it cannot be
explained: the happiness of being at one with everything in that
hidden ground of Love for which there can be no explanations.
(The Hidden Ground of Love, *p. 115*)

For God's love is like a river springing up in the depths of the
Divine Substance and flowing endlessly through His creation,
filling all things with life and goodness and strength. (New
Seeds of Contemplation, *p. 266*)

I wrote earlier about the need of a concordance of the Merton
vocabulary and I mused on what words might have the
largest number of references. I suggested that
"contemplation" would be near the top. So, too, would the
word "God." In his book, *The Silent Life*, Merton describes the
monk as one who "devotes his entire life to seeking God."
While this search for God may appear more evident in the life
of the monk, it is, in ultimate terms, the goal of everyone.
Saint Augustine was describing the human condition when
he prayed to God in his *Confessions*: "Our hearts are restless
until they find their rest in Thee." Merton expresses this in
his own way in a moving chapter in *New Seeds of*
Contemplation, wherein he describes a fractured humanity
being made one by the love of God. In another chapter
entitled "A Body of Broken Bones," he speaks of God's love
as "the resetting of a Body of broken bones" (p. 72). In yet
another comparison in that same chapter he calls God "a

consuming Fire," wanting to rid us of all that seems to separate us from the Divine Self. "As long as we do not permit His love to consume us entirely and to unite us in Himself, the gold that is in us will be hidden by the rock and dirt which keep us separate from one another" (p. 70).

At this point, as we begin talking about God, I need to sound an important warning: We must be careful how we speak of seeking God. It's not the same as seeking some object, say, a new car or a new house. We must not reduce God to the status of an "object" or a "thing," as if God were something that could be grasped and possessed in the way we possess riches or knowledge or some other created entity. Nor must we seek God outside ourselves. (Remember Merton's words, quoted above, which describe prayer as "the response to God within us, the discovery of God within us.")

For God is not an "object" or a "thing." God's infinity, as the word implies, knows no boundaries; hence we cannot "define" God as we define things in the world. "His presence cannot be verified as we would verify a laboratory experiment" (*Contemplative Prayer*, p. 79). If you were to line up all the beings that exist or ever have existed, God would not be one of them. This is to say God is not one of the beings God created. Rather God is the Source from which all beings derive and the Ground in which they are continually sustained.

In a letter to a young Indian student studying at the University in Cracow, Poland, Merton writes of the naive atheism of nineteenth-century scientism:

> They think that religious people believe in a God who is simply a "being" among other beings, part of a series of beings, an "object" which can be discovered and demonstrated. This of course is a false notion of God, the Absolute, the source and origin of all Being, beyond all beings and transcending them all and hence not to be sought as one among them. (*The Hidden Ground of Love*, p. 452)

As soon as we try to verify God's presence as an object of exact knowledge, God eludes us.

Now if God is not to be sought among the beings we know in this life, it follows that *we cannot know God as we know created beings*. That makes sense, does it not? Yet at the same time it is true that *what we know about God we can know only through created beings*. For created beings, insofar as they are real, participate in a limited way in the qualities and perfections of the One who alone is Absolutely Real. There is, as it were, "something of God" in every creature that exists. In experiencing creatures, we experience that "something of God."

The words we use to describe creatures, therefore, can serve as metaphors or symbols that enable us to have some knowledge of God. As I write this, I can look out the window of my office and through that window I can get some very limited understanding of the universe. Compared to the immensity of the universe, what I know by looking out that window is practically nothing. Even if I looked through many windows and in different directions, the knowledge of the universe I would attain would still be skimpy at best. Modern technology has made it possible for astronauts to see the earth from out in space. Even that is meager knowledge compared to the entire universe and, while their knowledge increases quantitatively (they see more), it decreases qualitatively (they see less clearly). They cannot from their place in space see the earth in the detail that I can see through my window.

The ideas, the concepts, the images, the symbols, the metaphors we use to describe God are like those windows through which we look out at the universe. They are images of created things which, because there is "something of God" in them, can tell us something *about* God. Thus, in the image we have of a person we call "father," we can see something of God and hence can speak of God as "father" (though I should add that some people have poor experiences of "father" and for this reason find it difficult to describe God as "father"). In someone we call "mother" we can also experience "something of God" and, therefore, we can use the name "mother" to describe God. And there are many other images we can use, lover, spouse, guide, helper, to name a few. In a certain sense we can say "the more the merrier," since each image, each concept, can give a different insight into the God whom we can never know in any total sort of way.

Our language about God, then, is always inadequate. One way of putting this is to say that our experience of God is continually outstripping what we are able to say about the experience. Listen to Merton: "[A]s soon as we light these small matches which are our concepts: 'intelligence,' 'love,' 'power,' the tremendous reality of God Who infinitely exceeds all concepts suddenly bears down upon us like a dark storm and blows out all their flames!" (*The Ascent to Truth*, p. 106).

At the same time we must not underestimate the value and importance of the rich imagery that the Bible and our culture offer us. The richer the imagery, the more deeply will we be able to know about God through God's creation. But let us be very clear: There is a huge difference between knowing *about* God through God's creation and knowing God as God is in the divine Self. Knowing *about* God is "mediated" knowledge, that is, we know God through an intermediary. This normally is what we think of when we speak of God. And some would say: This is enough. Short of heaven and the beatific vision, we can only know God through the medium of the creatures God has made.

But there is a long tradition, the contemplative or mystical tradition—a tradition that was most congenial to Thomas Merton's approach to spirituality—which claims that we can know God *immediately*. This is to say that we can know the divine reality as It is in Itself, and not simply through the medium of images, metaphors, ideas, concepts. But to do this we have to turn off the lights of our mind, that is, we have to go beyond concepts and ideas. This means going into darkness. For when you turn off light you are in darkness. It also means going beyond words that would try to describe God. But to go beyond words is to go into silence. In darkness and silence the only light we have is faith, whereby we grasp God or rather are grasped by God. This means that the way of Faith is the way of Love. It is God's love that grasps us and our love, moved by grace, that seeks to grasp God. Thus, when all our concepts and images admit that they cannot really know God, love cries out: "I know God!"

To put this another way, in contemplation we come to know that our very being is penetrated through and through with God's love. God is the hidden ground of love in all that is. Hence, as Merton puts it:

> Our knowledge of God is paradoxically a knowledge not of God as the object of our scrutiny, but of ourselves as utterly dependent on his saving and merciful knowledge of us.... We know him in and through ourselves in so far as his truth is the source of our being and his merciful love is the very heart of our life and existence. (*Contemplative Prayer*, p. 83)

Knowing God in the darkness of a love that goes beyond all that human reason can know is the greatest joy and happiness possible in this life. Yet the very experience of "knowing in darkness," "knowing without knowing," begets the yearning for that moment of total transformation, when we shall see God face-to-face.

For Merton coming to know God is intimately linked with coming to know myself in my true identity. Hence we turn now to the theme of human identity.

～～～～～～ 4. Human Identity ～～～～～～

The human soul is still the image of God, and no matter how far it travels away from Him into the regions of unreality, it never becomes so completely unreal that its original destiny can cease to torment it with a need to return to itself in God, and become, once again, real. (The New Man, p. 112)

Now if we take our vulnerable shell to be our true identity, if we think our mask is our true face, we will protect it with fabrications even at the cost of violating our own truth...until in the end we have the enormous, obsessive, uncontrollable dynamic of fabrications designed to protect mere fictitious identities—

"selves," that is to say, regarded as objects. Selves that can stand back and see themselves having fun (an illusion which reassures them that they are real). (Raids on the Unspeakable, *p. 15*)

Sad indeed is the case of that exterior self that imagines himself contemplative, and seeks to achieve contemplation as the fruit of planned effort and of spiritual ambition. He will assume varied attitudes, and meditate on the inner significance of his own postures and try to fabricate for himself a contemplative identity; and all the while there is nobody there....

The inner self is as secret as God and, like Him, it evades every concept that tries to seize hold of it with full possession. It is a life that cannot be held and studied as object, because it is not "a thing." ("The Inner Experience," in Thomas Merton: Spiritual Master, *pp. 297-298)*

Since we find our identity only in God, the next gallery room to move into is the one marked: "Self Identity." One of the consistent themes that weaves its way through much of Merton's writings is precisely the human search for self-identity. He is very clear that one's true identity is not that which appears on the surface. There is a huge difference between what we appear to be and what we are, between our exterior self and our inner self. The exterior self, which we think ourselves to be and which we show to others, is not the deep interior self that alone is real. My great spiritual task, therefore, is to lose my self (my exterior self) in order to find myself (my inner or true self). This is the gospel paradox: We must lose ourselves (our false selves) in order to find ourselves (our true selves). And the only "place" where we can find our true self is in God.

We come from God and must return to God. And the return to God is a journey. On the journey there are two forces at work in us: (1) a *centrifugal* force that carries us away from our true identity (and therefore from God), and (2) a *centripetal* force, which is God's gift returning us to that identity. The centrifugal force is what we name original sin: It is that in us which *draws us away from our center* into regions of unreality. It propels us to build up a superficial, even illusory ego that ultimately is without substance. The centripetal force, on the other hand, is the power of the Spirit of God *drawing us to our center,* where we find God and in God we discover (or, rather, recover) our own true selves.

As you read what Merton has to say about spirituality, you will find two terms recurring: exterior or false self and the inner or true self (I referred briefly to them in talking about contemplation). He uses a variety of terms to describe these entities. Though I don't want to tire you out with long lists, I do believe that enumerating some of these variants can help us understand what Merton meant when he used these rather elusive terms. Thus, among the terms he uses for the exterior self, are the following:

superficial self (*New Seeds of Contemplation,* pp. 7, 11, 16)

empirical self (Ibid., pp. 7, 11, 279)

outward self (Ibid., pp. 7, 21)

shadow self (Ibid., p. 109)

smoke self (Ibid., p. 38)

contingent self (Ibid., p. 38)

imaginary self (Ibid., p. 57)

private self (Ibid., p. 34)

illusory self (Ibid., p. 281)

false self (Ibid., pp. 21, 25, 26, 33, 34)

petty self (*Monastic Journey,* p. 40)

These various descriptive adjectives are, to say the least, not very flattering. I would not welcome them as descriptions of the self that I want to be. But, of course, this is precisely the point: These terms do not describe my true self. In a sense they hide my true self. To quote Merton:

> Every one of us is shadowed by an illusory person: a false self.... My false and private self is the one who wants to exist outside the reach of God's will and God's love—outside of reality and outside of life. And such a self cannot

help but be an illusion.... For most of the people in the
world, there is no greater subjective reality than this false
self of theirs, which cannot exist. (*New Seeds of
Contemplation*, p. 34)

For the true self Merton also has a number of very different,
descriptive terms:

inner self (*New Seeds of Contemplation*, p. 279)

hidden self (Ibid.)

creative, mysterious inner self (Ibid., p. 38)

inmost self (Ibid., p. 282)

real self (*Conjectures of a Guilty Bystander*, p. 134)

deepest, most hidden self (Ibid., p. 166)

These synonyms are much more welcome, don't you think? I
find it exciting to think of these terms in reference to myself
and to my friends and acquaintances. They express
hiddenness, mystery, innerness, depth, reality. They invite
exploration. They make me realize how little I know of my
real self and that of others, how much more I have yet to
learn.

The External Self

From what I have already said, it can be seen that the external
self is a human construct that we bring into being by our own
actions, especially our habits of selfishness and our constant
flight from reality. It is an empty self. Out of touch with my
inner reality, it is the complex in me of all that is not God and,
therefore, all that is ultimately destined to disappear. It is, in
Merton's phrase, like smoke going up a chimney. Because it
exists at the surface level of reality, it is incapable of any kind
of transcendent experience, which is to say that it cannot
know God. It has a history and a biography, both of which
end at death.

The True Self

The true self, on the other hand, is the self that sleeps silently in my depths, waiting to be awakened by the power of the Spirit. It is the openness in us to the call of God to become one with God (or rather to discover that we are and always have been one with God). It is what Daniel Walsh, Merton's onetime teacher and friend, called "man's capacity for divinity," and what the distinguished German Catholic theologian, Karl Rahner, called the human "openness to the Transcendent." Merton describes it as "the white-hot point of mystical receptivity" (*The New Man*, p. 208), which is present in all of us, but dormant in most of us.

I am quite conscious, dear reader, that all this is difficult to grasp. The trouble is quite frankly that the true self cannot really be described or even reflected upon. *The true self is our own subjectivity which can never be known as an object or a thing.* In other words, it makes no sense to think of the true self knowing itself as an object distinct from itself. For an object distinct from the true self would not be the true self. It is something like the paradox: We see with our eyes, yet we cannot see our eyes. What I mean by this analogy is this: We can see objects with our eyes, but our eyes can never be objects that we are able to see. Just so, the true self is not an entity we are able to know at the level of ordinary human consciousness. It cannot be known, but it can be experienced—though only at a level of consciousness deeper than that which we normally reach.

Awakening to the Deepest Ground of Our Being

Whereas the external self, created as it is by our own egocentric desires and our efforts to manipulate or to allow ourselves to be manipulated, is ever in process of coming into existence (though always at a superficial level of being), the true self is always there as God's invitation to become identified with the Divine Self. It is the insistent voice of God's Spirit, calling us to be reborn, awakening us to the deepest ground of our being. It is a deep spiritual consciousness. Merton describes it as "the insatiable diamond of spiritual awareness."

When this spiritual awareness takes hold in our lives, all sorts of wondrous things begin to happen. Having reached the level of consciousness where we are aware that we are in God and that the true self of everyone is in God, our relationships are inevitably transformed. We perceive the whole human family as one and this intuition begins to govern everything we do.◄

Not Three Entities

One of the problems I face when I talk about my true self and my false self is that I seem to be talking about three different entities: namely, myself and the two selves that I have, that is, the false self and the true self. But to make this threefold distinction is to miss completely the point of what we are discussing. The true self is myself. It is who I really am. It expresses my identity which I can find only in God. The false self, on the other hand, is, in ultimate terms, an illusion. We can carry it around with us as long as we will, but it cannot survive death. Indeed, the way to understand death is not as the separation of the soul from the body, but as the disappearance of the external self and the emergence of the true self. In death I find myself in God.

Death as the Emergence of the True Self

This is the lot of most people: Death becomes the ultimate affirmation of their true identity. This emergence of the true self in death is a discovery of a oneness not only with God but in God with others. As Merton writes:

> We do not finally taste the full exultation of God's glory until we share His infinite gift of it by overflowing and transmitting glory all over heaven, and seeing God in all the others who are there, and knowing that He is the Life of all of us and that we are all One in Him. (*New Seeds of Contemplation*, pp. 65-66)

Our society desperately needs a more positive attitude toward what Emily Dickinson calls "death's tremendous nearness." Death is not the end of a contest where prizes or penalties are handed out to winners and losers. Death is going home, to the only home that can satisfy our deepest longings and desires. Death is God's response to the words of Augustine which I have already quoted: "Our hearts are restless till they find their rest in Thee."

I truly believe that God is present with the dying person and doing things we can never discern. The superficialities of life get cast aside. A false self is sloughed off and one's true self appears. When a person lapses into unconsciousness, that person is not just "out of it." The individual may be very much into it. Thomas Merton once wrote to a friend: "All that is best is unconscious or superconscious." What he means is that there is—as I mentioned earlier—about us and around us a vast area of the unconscious that is rarely explored; or when it is explored, this is done only at a psychological level. Yet there is a spiritual level to the unconscious that puts one in touch with realities of the spirit that go far beyond the realities of this life.

Deeper Consciousness as We Approach Death

I believe that, as we move closer to death, we come to realize more and more our real self that for so long a time has been overshadowed by a false self. I recall a very vivid experience I had with an aunt of mine, Florence Gilbert, who died at a nursing home in Rochester, New York. I used to visit her regularly. One day I noticed on her dresser a photograph. It was that of a strikingly beautiful woman. On the photograph was written "Happy Birthday, Dad, 1930, from Florence." I took the photo and had it framed. Then I asked a workman at the home if they would put it on the wall in a place where she could view it. They did. The next time I went to visit her, I pointed to the photo and asked her: "Who is that beautiful woman in the photograph?" She answered: "I don't know." Then I said: "That is you." There was disbelief in her eyes:

"No," she said firmly, "that's not me."

From then on it became a kind of ritual each time I visited. I would ask the question. She would say she didn't know who it was. I would say: "It's you." She would deny it. This went on for some months.

Then one day when I visited her, it was clear that she would not live much longer. But I continued our little game. Yet again I asked her: "Who is that beautiful woman in the photograph?" She looked at me. A big grin came over her face. She said: "That's me."

I truly believe that this was a change in consciousness that came to her. She was no longer an aged woman whose body showed the ravages of time. She was beginning to experience her true self, the self in each one of us that is known only to God. She had caught a glimpse of that eternal youth and eternal beauty that awaited her. The photo became an icon of eternity.

Death as 'Yes' to God

In death one is face-to-face with God, with Ultimate Reality. All the things that might distract us (act as *divertissement*) in this life are gone. If all through life we have tried to affirm our true identity (speaking a "yes" to God that was sometimes firm, sometimes hesitant), all the things that might lead us away from God have disappeared. There is nothing to prevent us from saying a resounding "yes." Death is that final "yes" we say to God and at the same time it is the most free. And we are home at last. We have found our identity, our true self.

Contemplation as the Emergence of the True Self

This side of death, it is possible to reach one's true self only in contemplation. In contemplation the false self recedes and the true self awakens. Contemplation is the journey from realms of unlikeness (to God), to realms of likeness. It is the journey from Egypt to the Promised Land. It is the return from exile to paradise. For, to Merton, the state of humans before the fall was contemplation. He sees the fall as a plunge from the unity of the contemplative life into the state of disunity and alienation in which we presently find ourselves. It is the fall from contemplation that brings into existence the fallen, alienated external self that wants to live in separateness and isolation and that, as a self-constructed illusion, attempts to take over the functions of the inner self.

This is not to say that the external self is evil, though it suffers the effects of sin. It can be involved in the external practices of religion. It can even desire to be a contemplative or to write books on contemplation. But the external self can never become truly contemplative. For contemplation is the union of myself with God and it is impossible to unite with God that which, in ultimate terms, is an illusion. As Merton writes:

> It is not enough to remain the same "self," the same individual ego, with a new set of activities and a new lot of religious practices. One must be born of the Spirit who is free, and who teaches the inmost depths of the heart by taking that heart to Himself, by making Himself one with our heart, by creating for us, invisibly, a new identity; by being Himself that identity. (*Honorable Reader*, p. 134)

Contemplation is possible only by going beyond the external self to the real self that is identified with God. Only then do I discover who I really am. The discovery is a return to my original identity that was never really lost, only hidden. "It is not," as Merton says, "that we discover a new unity. We recover an older unity" (*The Asian Journal*, p. 308). Thus, in contemplation, I do not become something that I was not; rather I become what I truly am. I become aware that in the depths of my being, I am, and always have been, contemplative.

Merton often equated the true self with the person and the false self with the individual, as we shall see in the next section.

⌒5. *Community (of Persons) vs. Collectivity (of Individuals)*⌒

The problem of Beranger in Ionesco's Rhinoceros *is the problem of the human person stranded and alone in what threatens to become a society of monsters. In the sixth century Beranger might perhaps have walked off into the desert of Scete (in Egypt) without too much concern over the fact that all his fellow citizens, all his friends, and even his girl Daisy, had turned into rhinoceroses.*

The problem today is that there are no deserts, only dude ranches. (Raids on the Unspeakable, *p. 19*)

[I]n reality, all men are solitary. Only most of them are so averse to being alone, or to feeling alone, that they do everything they can to forget their solitude. How? Perhaps in large measure by what Pascal called "divertissement"—diversion, systematic distraction. By those occupations and recreations, so mercifully provided by society, which enable a man to avoid his own company for twenty-four hours a day. (Disputed Questions, *p. 178*)

The person must be rescued from the individual. The free son of God must be saved from the conformist slave of fantasy, passion and convention. The creative and mysterious inner self must be delivered from the wasteful, hedonistic and destructive ego that seeks only to cover itself with disguises. (New Seeds of Contemplation, *p. 38*)

Moving about the Merton Gallery we come upon rooms with large windows gazing outward to a world for which we must take responsibility. We are speaking now about Merton in the last decade of his life. As he entered that decade, he saw the world in a way that was radically different from the world view he had embraced when in 1941 he had entered the Abbey of Our Lady of Gethsemani. One way of expressing his thinking at the beginning of the 1960's is to say that he had moved away from the simplistic view of the world, so evident in *The Seven Storey Mountain,* in which the world is divided into a monastic world and a secular world. Now what he saw was a world in which men and women were faced with one of two choices: either a society of *persons* conscious of community and communion, or a society of isolated *individuals* drowned in the nameless isolation and the unredeemed alienation of collectivity. And what was going on before people's very eyes was the mighty pull of a technology drawing them relentlessly in the direction of the collectivity and away from the community.

More and more Merton comes to understand that the real struggle in human life is the struggle to construct the human community—with its values of human dignity, human freedom, solitude and contemplation. The alternative to this struggle is to be absorbed almost helplessly into the collectivity, in which men and women give up their freedom of thought and action and become part of the system that controls them and all of human life.

This contrast between the community (the place of freedom) and the collectivity (the place of slavery) is, at least implicitly if not always explicitly, a constant theme in Merton's writings in the 1960's. Closely linked with this contrast is the difference between the person (the true self) and the individual (the false self). The person is the man or woman who lives in community; the individual is the man or woman who is isolated in collectivity. The individual is simply a unit divided off from all other units. He or she is a single separate being, definable only in a negative way: He or she is not "someone else." "Individuals" live in isolation and alienation from one another. They are united only superficially by an external uniformity that has scarcely any relationship to the inner realities of the human spirit. The collectivity is the mass-society that is constructed out of these disconnected individuals or, to use Merton's words, "out of empty and alienated human beings who have lost their center and extinguished their own inner light in order to depend in abject passivity upon the mass in which they cohere without affectivity or intelligent purpose" (*Disputed Questions*, p. x).

Far different from the "individual" is the "person" who is a center of freedom and love, linked with brothers and sisters in the unity of all that makes them human and in a sharing of all that makes them one in Christ. Whereas the individual is absorbed in the *stereotype*, the person is conformed to the *archetype* who is Christ. For Merton the fullness of personhood and the meaning of community is "to be in Christ." Merton would want to say with Saint Paul: "Now it is not I [that is the isolated individual] but Christ [that is, the person linked together with other persons in the archetype of all humanity] who lives in me."

Persons find in the community the place for solitude and therefore for contemplation. The collectivity, on the other hand, is the place of what the seventeenth-century French philosopher Blaise Pascal calls *"divertissement,"* an untranslatable word which roughly means "distraction" or "diversion": It is the escape from life's problems, and also its invitations, into activities that in ultimate terms are meaningless. It is a constant turning to superficial actions as a way to avoid facing the true realities of human life. The soap operas and situation comedies easily become an addiction. They take the place of the "bread and circuses" of ancient Rome. There was plenty wrong with Roman society and the Roman emperors offered the diversion of food and entertainment to make people forget the banality and meaninglessness of the lives they lived. Our society does much the same and has ever so much more in the way of sophisticated tools for doing so.

People whose lives are shaped by the collectivity are people who have lost their sense of the transcendent. This means that they are deprived of their natural capacity for contemplation. In an essay that has become something of a classic ("Rain and the Rhinoceros" in *Raids on the Unspeakable*) Merton describes the sickness of this mass-society that has lost its sense of solitude and its capacity for contemplation. He calls it "rhinoceritis." He is drawing on Eugene Ionesco's powerful play *Rhinoceros* to illustrate what he means by the collectivity. In this play, everyone except the character Beranger becomes a victim of "rhinoceritis." This is a disease which consists in compliance with whatever is the norm of the moment, no matter how absurd it may be.

Rhinoceros opens in a small French village. Two people sit at an outdoor cafe having their morning coffee. All at once they see a herd of rhinoceroses racing through the main street. As they look in the direction from which the herd has come, they see people coming out of their houses, joining the herd and being transformed into rhinoceroses. As the herd rushes by them, they feel the strong urge to join. Finally one of them does. And Beranger is left as the last human being on earth, the last person. He, too, feels a strong urge to abandon his humanness and join the herd, but something deep in him prevents him from doing so. He persists in remaining human in what has become a nonhuman world.

One of the responsibilities that Merton sees for himself and other contemplatives in society is to call for more "Berangers" to face up to the fatuity of the collectivity's illusory priorities and to renounce the "mass mind" so that they may once again become true persons and be in touch with what is real. Merton quotes Ionesco as saying that there will always be a place "for those isolated consciences which have stood up for the universal conscience" as against the "mass mind." Merton adds: "But their place is solitude. They have no other. Hence it is the solitary person (whether in the city or in the desert) who does mankind the inestimable favor of reminding it of its true capacity for maturity, liberty and peace" (*Raids on the Unspeakable*, p. 220).

Ionesco himself has made the same point, that only the solitude which is proper to the community can save people from the slavery of unthinking conformism. Thus he writes: "Forms of rhinoceritis of every kind, from left and right, are there to threaten humanity when men [and women] have no time to think or collect themselves; and they lie in wait for mankind today, because we have lost all feeling and taste for genuine solitude. For solitude is not *separation* but *mediation*...." (Ionesco, *Notes and Counter Notes: Writings on the Theatre*, trans. Donald Watson [New York: Grove Press, 1964], p. 151).

At this point I need to make clear that it would surely be a misunderstanding to think that either the community or the collectivity exists in a pure state. There is a bit of each in all of us. This was also true of Merton and he would have been the first to admit it. Our Christian task is to expose—in ourselves as well as in our society—the illusions that the collectivity lives by and to work for the building up of the community.

⌁⌁ 6. *Freedom as the Expression of One's Inner Truth* ⌁⌁

Perfect spiritual freedom is a total inability to make any evil choice. (New Seeds of Contemplation, *p. 199*)

It is our liberty that makes us Persons, constituted in the divine image.... [T]he Church has, as one of its chief functions, the preservation of our spiritual liberty as [children] of God. How few people realize this! (Ibid., *p. 202*)

The real inner life and freedom of man begin when this inner dimension opens up and man lives in communion with the unknown within him. On the basis of this he can also be in communion with the same unknown in others. (Witness to Freedom, *pp. 329-330*)

Here we may enter the gallery room marked "Freedom." In *Witness to Freedom*, the fifth and final volume of the collected Merton letters, I have indicated three stages in Merton's growth to freedom. First, there was that early stage—his youthful years—when freedom meant for him doing whatever he wanted to do (though many times during that period he was not really sure what it was that he wanted to do). If you will, it was freedom that liberated him, as far as possible, from rules and regulations that would prevent him from following the whim or desire of the moment. It was a pseudo-freedom, a freedom without discipline of any sort.

The second stage in Merton's journey to true and authentic freedom came in his mid-twenties. It was far better than stage one, but still a fairly limited experience of freedom. It finds its best expression perhaps in the words he used to describe the night he arrived at Gethsemani to become a monk. He tells us that Brother Matthew closed the gate behind him and he was enclosed in the *four walls of his new freedom*. It certainly was a new freedom, but his articulation of it is a rather curious way of defining freedom: enclosure within four walls. In this second period of his journey to true and authentic freedom, Merton saw freedom as an inner power, but one that was largely directed from the outside. It was the form of freedom that existed so long in religious communities: a freedom that meant obedience to the Rule that governed that community and to the superiors who administered and interpreted that Rule.

If stage one was unbridled freedom that liberated him *from the observance of rules*, stage two amounted to a freedom that liberated him (so he believed at the time) *through the observance of the rules*. The mentality in the monastery when he entered in 1941 was quite simple: Observe the Rule and you are safe with God. Observe the rules prescribed for you, obey the directives of your superiors and you are exercising your freedom in a way that is pleasing to God.

A Deeper Understanding of Freedom

These two stages of freedom are fairly uncomplicated and easily understood. The third stage of freedom, which Merton embraced as he grew in his understanding of the monastic life and especially as contemplative spirituality came more and more to influence everything that he did—this is more difficult to explain and to understand. It is a stage in which freedom becomes more and more interiorized. It is the freedom whereby I respond to my own inner truth, my own inner unity, my own spiritual center.

This stage of freedom is possible only for someone who has entered into a deep contact with what is truly real: the reality of God, the reality of oneself, the reality of all God's creation. The road that leads to this kind of freedom is strewn with many fallen idols: the false God, the false self, the false image of God's creatures. I become free only when I have unmasked the illusions that falsify my vision of what is. I become free only when I see all of reality as it really is.

If I wish to take the road toward this kind of true freedom, I must manage somehow to build that quiet time and that contemplative dimension, which I discussed above, into my life, so that I live more on the inside than on the outside. This living on the inside involves a process of creating (or better discovering) a center and a focus for the divergent elements of my being. Moving in this direction, I become increasingly able to see my life as one unified whole, not as a fragmented existence in which I am being pulled in so many directions and by so many claims on my attention that I do not know where I am going or even who it is that goes.

As I continue to unify and simply my life (and, I repeat, this requires quiet time, prayer, personal discipline in my life), I reach a point where I begin to see reality as it truly is, uncolored by ambition, greed or the passion to control and manipulate. I begin to see the "Real" in all that is "real." Or to use a Zen expression, I become free to see people and objects "without affirmation or denial." This is important, for when I become judgmental about persons and objects, what happens? I do not really see things as they are. Rather I see what I project on them instead of what is there.

This is not to say that I never make judgments in my life. On the contrary, making judgments is an important element of freedom. But I must avoid "prejudices," which are pre-judgments, that is, judgments that are already in place before I look at who or what is there. I cannot "just see" a person, if in the very gesture of looking at that person, I see her or him as an object to be used or manipulated for my own self-serving purposes. I cannot "just see" things, if I always view them from a perspective that is pragmatic and utilitarian. In his unpublished book "The Inner Experience" Merton offers a helpful example. He draws a contrast between a child's vision of a tree and a lumberman's vision.

> The child sees the tree in a way that is utterly simple and uncolored by ulterior motives. The lumberman, when he sees a tree, may be aware of its beauty, but his vision is conditioned by motives of profit and conditions of business. He cannot just "see" the tree.

The more I am able to see persons and things as they are, the more liberated I become. It becomes increasingly possible for me to be my true self. I acquire the ability to say my own "yes" or "no" and put my whole self into the saying of it.

This is not to say that freedom means the elimination of control in my life. True freedom cannot be an aimless drifting in realms of indecision. On the contrary, it presupposes control, but a control that is self-directed. It is immanent and personal, not external and manipulative. Freedom is never capricious. It is not so much doing as I want as wanting what I do and knowing at the very center of my being why I want to do it.

Freedom, in other words, is the power of responding to my own inner truth. The expression "inner truth," which Merton frequently uses to describe that center, where I find myself and God and the unity of all that is, is closely akin to a term used by contemporary moralists, namely, the fundamental option. (I should say this rather quietly, for a few Catholic theologians do not like this term. The reason they dislike it is, I believe, their failure to understand what it really means.)

Fundamental Option

The fundamental option, as understood by moralists today, represents that accumulation of values and principles that a person has so appropriated and made his or her own that they become a unifying force in a person. They create a unity in that person's life from which the person's actions flow and from which his or her life takes direction.

Responding to my inner truth is saying "yes" to God and to my own identity realized in God. It is saying "no" to all that is illusory, false and less then human. The "yes" or "no" which I utter must be internal before it is externalized. A "yes" or a "no" that is purely external, because it is imposed on me from the outside, is not really mine and therefore not free. When one's actions are dictated by "the system"— whether that system be the state, the party or even the

Church—one's freedom is wounded at its very core.

I am in no way denying a certain precariousness involved in following one's own inner truth. I am not infallible and I can be wrong. To use Merton's words:

> The most difficult kind of ethic is the kind which impels you to follow what seems to be your own inner truth. And of course, you always make plenty of mistakes that way. But that is the point. I cease to understand any reason for wanting to be always right. It is so hard to do the one thing that matters, which is to be not right, but sincere. And what a difference! The Grand Inquisitors are afraid of such an approach.... (*The Hidden Ground of Love*, pp. 392-393)

Freedom and Authority

Freedom, therefore, is not incompatible with authority. Authority properly exercised can offer authentic guidelines that can help me respond to my inner truth. Since freedom is exercised in community, where my decisions must interact with the decisions of other people, authority can be helpful in clarifying the concrete ways in which this interaction of decisions can serve and promote the common good of all. Thus, authority, when it respects my inner truth, can enhance my freedom: for it helps me to exercise it wisely.

On the other hand, freedom is not compatible with authoritarianism. Authoritarianism is authority acting with naked power. Authority degenerates into authoritarianism when it imposes its dictates without dialogue and without regard for the inner truth of the subjects of that authority. One expects to find authoritarianism in institutions that are totalitarian in character. It is surely surprising—though unfortunately not an uncommon experience—to find it in institutions that should by their very nature be committed to fostering and preserving freedom. Much of Merton's writings in his later years show a deep concern to unmask elements of unfreedom existing in American society, in monasticism and also in the Church.

In the holographic Notebook Number 35, under the date

May 24, 1968, Merton discusses three ways of freedom described by Herbert Marcuse, the Berlin-born American Marxist philosopher. Taking a lead from Marcuse's ideas, Merton suggests that the life of a free person might be described as a life of poverty, chastity and obedience. Since it empties my heart of false desires and illusory self-seeking, freedom is a *poverty* of spirit that liberates me from enslavement to the false needs that a consumer society imposes on me through the subtle powers of the mass media.

By keeping me clearheaded and single-minded, freedom becomes a *chastity* of mind that enables me to see beyond the maze of indoctrination with which public opinion attempts to becloud my vision of reality. Such chastity of mind makes it possible for me to take a critical stance toward the spurious values and empty concerns that people often mistake for reality.

Finally, freedom begets an *obedience* to the Holy Spirit that puts me in touch with the authentic movements of the human spirit stirring in today's world and seeking, often against great odds, to affirm the most basic human values and to call all men and women to recover the integrity of their inner depths. ❧

Freedom of Spontaneity

To be a bit pedantic (if I have not already been so), I want to say that it should be clear that the freedom Merton speaks of is the freedom of *spontaneity*, not the freedom of *contrariety*. What philosophers call the freedom of contrariety means the power to choose the good or the bad. It means being able to say "yes" or "no" to God. What we need to realize is that choosing the bad or saying "no" to God is not really freedom at all. It is slavery. For to choose the bad as if it were good is to fail to see things as they really are. It is therefore an illusory freedom. To say "no" to God is not really an exercise of freedom, but rather an exercise in futility and stupidity. For it is saying "no" to that which alone sustains me in existence. The only true freedom is that which spontaneously moves toward the good. This is what I mean by freedom of spontaneity.

Sin is a form of unfreedom. Sin is much more than the breaking of an external law. It is a failure to respond to my inner truth. It is the will to do what God does not will. It is saying "yes," when my inner truth calls me to say "no," and "no" when it calls me to say "yes." Sin is delusion in the literal sense of the word *deludere*, which means "to play false with." It is playing the game of life falsely. I not only do what is false. I become, in a sense, a false being. As Merton writes in *The Inner Experience*, in sin I experience an inner falsity which "tells me not merely that I have done wrong, but that I *am* wrong, through and through."

Besides sin, which is unfreedom because it is an abuse of true freedom, there is another form of unfreedom. This is the unfreedom that comes from forces outside me that violate my freedom and prevent me from exercising it. This is unfreedom that comes from coercion.

In the 1960's, Thomas Merton wrote a great deal about the unfreedom that comes from coercion. As he acquired in his solitude a deeper compassion for people, his concern went out to all who were oppressed by war and violence, by false political and economic ideologies, by social injustices and tyrannical structures. He saw clearly the link between war and huge industrial complexes who quite literally cannot afford peace, for they gain such tremendous profit from the war industries.

Merton gave active support to the Catholic Peace Movement and the Catholic Worker group. He was one of the first Catholics to become a member of the Fellowship of Reconciliation, which he joined in 1962. He encouraged the Berrigans in their opposition to war (though he did not always agree with their tactics). He became a close friend of the late John Howard Griffin and a collaborator with him in the struggle for civil rights. He had deep respect for the Rev. Dr. Martin Luther King, Jr., and in fact was awaiting a visit from him when the tragic news came of his assassination.

He admired Mohandas Gandhi and in his short book

Gandhi on Non-violence he proposed the thinking and tactics of this great Indian leader as a model for American activists. Like Gandhi he saw the essential relationship between nonviolence and any authentic renewal of society. "The only real liberation," he wrote, "is that which *liberates both the oppressor and the oppressed* at the same time from the tyrannical automatism of the violent process" (p. 14). Like Gandhi, Merton believed that the efficacy of nonviolence was to be judged, not by immediate results, but by the commitment to truth and love.

Though he remained in his monastery, Merton seemed to be everywhere by his compassion and concern. Steadfastly and firmly he resisted the urgings of those who wanted him to leave the cloister and join them in the front lines of battle against the "principalities and powers." He never wavered in the belief that being in the monastery gave him the right distance from the "world": a place that enabled him to explore and discover "new dimensions of freedom" (*Contemplation in a World of Action*, p. 178). In his letter on the contemplative life, written at the behest of Pope Paul VI, Merton quoted the Islamic statement: "The hen does not lay eggs in the marketplace." More and more he looked on his monastery, not as a home where he was rooted and established, but as a place from which he could in some sense be everywhere. In the introduction to the Japanese edition of *The Seven Storey Mountain*, he wrote: "I disappear from the world as an object of interest in order to be everywhere in it by hiddenness and compassion" (*Honorable Reader*, p. 65).

The monastic life, he believed, is, or at least ought to be, an eschatological witness to the perfection of freedom, not realizable in this life. At the same time, the monastic life should be a sign witnessing to the hope of a better future for those whose freedom has been curtailed or destroyed by the forces of oppression and violence. The monastic life should be a beacon of light shining in the darkness of a violent world and calling all men and women to work that hope of a better future might become a reality for all God's people.

In an apocalyptic statement that echoes the strictures of

the Hebrew prophets against the inequalities and injustices of their times, Merton takes his stand with the poor, the oppressed and the victimized. In that same preface to the Japanese edition of *The Seven Storey Mountain*, he writes:

> It is my intention to make my entire life a rejection of, a protest against the crimes and injustices of war and political tyranny which threaten to destroy the whole [human] race...and the world with [it]. By my monastic life and vows I am saying NO to all the concentration camps, the aerial bombardments, the staged political trials, the judicial murders, the racial injustices, the economic tyrannies, and the whole socio-economic apparatus which seems geared for nothing but global destruction in spite of all its fair words in favor of peace. I make my monastic silence a protest against the lies of politicians, propagandists and agitators, and when I speak it is to deny that my faith and my Church can ever seriously be aligned with these forces of injustice and destruction. But it is true, nevertheless, that the faith in which I believe is also invoked by many who believe in war, believe in racial injustices, believe in self-righteous and lying forms of tyranny. My life must, then, be a protest against these also, and perhaps against these most of all (pp. 65-66).

People often ask the question: What would Merton's attitude be on the world situation today? I suspect it would be very much in keeping with the words of his I have just quoted. For they are words that come from his deepest center.

~~~~~~~~~~ 7. Nonviolence ~~~~~~~~~~

We are violent to others because we are already divided by the inner violence of our infidelity to our own truth. Hatred projects this division outside ourselves into society. (Conjectures of a Guilty Bystander, *p. 85*)

Without indifference to immediate fruits, nonviolence is powerless. (Witness to Freedom, *p. 284*)

I do not realize how strident I have been until I get into print.

The one in this month's Jubilee...*[May 1962] will set a whole lot of people right on their ear, and I guess it is my fault. I could after all have been more circumspect and moderate, and there are smoother ways of saying the same thing. I lash out with a baseball bat. Some professor of nonviolence I am.* (The Hidden Ground of Love, *p. 211*)

What I have just said about freedom moves us into another room in the gallery—a room whose contents were such that they surprised and even upset many who had been his faithful readers for at least a decade. For in 1961, much to the astonishment of the many people who had admired him for all he had said on prayer, Thomas Merton seemed suddenly to be turning to politics, writing about war and other social issues, challenging his readers to responsibility and action. The "rebel" was speaking out. And in monk's clothing. Many of his faithful followers were scandalized and bewildered by this change of direction. He had written so eloquently (they felt) about the sacred. Why is he suddenly turning to the secular? What do such things as conflict and war have to do with contemplation?

Contemplation and Social Issues

For the Merton of the 1960's, contemplation had a great deal to do with the social issues that troubled America and the world. If contemplation brings me (as inevitably it must) to an awareness of my oneness with God and in God my oneness with all God's creatures, then the things that trouble America and the world must necessarily be of concern to me. To Daniel Berrigan he wrote on June 25, 1963: "What is the contemplative life if one doesn't listen to God in it? What is the contemplative life if one becomes oblivious to the rights of men and the truth of God in the world and in His Church?" (*The Hidden Ground of Love*, p. 79)

Catholic Worker Article

Merton's initial entry into the social arena against war came with an article on war published in the October 1961 issue of *The Catholic Worker*. The article he sent to the *Worker* was actually a chapter from the manuscript of *New Seeds of Contemplation*, called "The Root of War Is Fear." To this book chapter he added three long paragraphs. These paragraphs had not been seen by the censors. Had the censors laid eyes on them, they probably would never have been published. Merton, whether naively or recklessly, made light of this "slight" omission, advising Dorothy Day that he had written them simply "to situate in the present crisis" what he had written in the book's chapter. As a matter of fact, these paragraphs were highly inflammatory. Deploring the war madness that had infected the whole world, he declared that no country was more afflicted with this madness than the United States. He challenged his fellow-Catholics, calling them to lead the way "on the road towards nonviolent settlement of difficulties and towards the gradual abolition of war as the way of settling international or civil disputes" (*Passion for Peace*, p. 12).

Note that the goal is "the abolition of war"; the means to achieve it, "nonviolence." He goes on to say:

> Christians must become active in every possible way.... there is much to be studied, much to be learned. Peace is to be preached, nonviolence is to be explained as a practical method.... Prayer and sacrifice must be used as the most effective spiritual weapons....we [must also be] willing to sacrifice and restrain our own instinct for violence and aggressiveness in our relations with other people.... It is the great Christian task of our time. (Ibid., pp. 12-13)

Satyagraha

Two years earlier, on July 9, 1959, he had written to Dorothy Day: "I am touched deeply by your witness for peace. You are very right in going at it along the lines of *Satyagraha*. I see no other way..." (*The Hidden Ground of Love*, p. 136). In 1964 he wrote, with even more urgency, to Olaf Anderson:

> We have to learn the lesson of *satyagraha* if we are to

preserve a meaningful human society on this earth. I am totally convinced of this. It is of absolutely primary importance. (*Witness to Freedom*, p. 105)

I have quoted twice Merton's use of the term *satyagraha* and you may perhaps be wondering: "What in the world does it mean?" Actually it is a Sanskrit word, coined by Mohandas Gandhi, to describe what had become for him a central idea in his struggle for the rights of Indians, first in South Africa, then in India. That central idea was a way of life and a tactic of action that struggled for justice, truth, love, peace, but without violence. Those committed to *satyagraha* are called *satyagrahis*. If you consult a good dictionary, you will find that *satyagraha* is a perfectly acceptable word. Yet I have to say that it is not a word that you would expect to hear at a cocktail party, much less at a football game or in a board of directors' meeting (unless it happened to be the board of a peace group).

The term Gandhi had originally employed to describe this kind of struggle was the Sanskrit word *ahimsa*, which means "noninjury." (*Himsa* means "injury." The alpha-privative [the "a"] negates the meaning of the noun and hence it literally means: noninjury, nonviolence.) Now to Gandhi, *ahimsa* was based on the spiritual truth of the unity of all reality and therefore meant something very positive. In literal translation, however, it loses this sense of unity which it had picked up from the culture in which it was used and, therefore, tends in translation to take on a negative meaning: not doing anything about evil.

Satyagraha, on the other hand, means holding on to the truth. Gandhi sometimes refers to it as truth-force or soul-force or love-force. But it should be clear that Gandhi intended this word to pick up all that is said and all that is implied in ahimsa. The pursuit of truth, he maintains, cannot mean inflicting injury or violence on one's opponent; but neither can it mean passivity, for an attitude of passivity means abandoning the pursuit of truth and ignoring the responsibility imposed on us by the unity of all reality.

Since the use of *satyagraha* seems a bit stilted and not

understood by many, we westerners who espouse *satyagraha* tend to use the word nonviolence to translate the meaning of the Sanskrit word. Not infrequently we face the same problem Gandhi had to deal with: Nonviolence, like *ahimsa*, sounds negative. One way of handling the problem is to refer to it as "active nonviolence" or, better still, to see "unconditional love" as a synonym for nonviolence.

Perhaps now we can return to the words Merton used in the inflammatory three-paragraph introduction to the article in the October 1961 issue of *The Catholic Worker*. You will remember his challenge to his readers to choose a nonviolent way of life. To this end nonviolence must be taught to people as a practical method toward settling difficulties, toward gradually abolishing war and toward overcoming our own instincts for violence and aggressiveness in our relations with other people. Much of what he wrote about war and peace in subsequent articles was an effort to explain nonviolence and the very positive meaning it is intended to evoke. ◆

What Brought Merton to Nonviolence?

The question naturally arises: Where did Merton get this notion that nonviolence was so important for true Christian living? The question has to be asked because he certainly did not find it in the Roman Catholic tradition of his time. There would have been no references to nonviolence in the moral theology text books of his day. For fifteen hundred years the attitude of the Catholic Church toward war was defined, not by nonviolence, but by the "just war" theory.[2] One would look in vain for any advocacy of nonviolence in Catholic writings on social issues in the 1960's. I studied at a Catholic seminary about the time Merton would have been studying moral theology as part of his preparation for ordination to the priesthood. That would have been in the 1940's. He would have used the same books as I had (the books that were standard fare in Catholic seminaries until after Vatican II). Nowhere did I ever see in my textbooks or ever hear in a classroom any mention of nonviolence, much less any discussion of it. By and large, American Catholics were a patriotic lot who felt that if America went to war, it must be a just one. They would have been suspicious of anyone who advocated nonviolence. The few who were brave enough to do so would have to wait till Vatican II's document on the Church in the Modern World (*Gaudium et Spes*) to find in a church document even a brief reference to nonviolence as a possible way to peace. And that document was not passed by the Council until 1965.

So the question persists: Where did Merton discover nonviolence and where did he get his deep conviction that it was crucially important for the future of the human race? I would like to say that he found it in the New Testament and in the teachings of Jesus. In actual fact, he (and a goodly number of other Christians besides) discovered nonviolence in the writings and in the life of Mohandas Gandhi; and it was from Gandhi that they derived the conviction that it was the only way that people could live together in peace. And Gandhi—where had he found nonviolence? In the teachings of Jesus Christ! Most especially in the Sermon on the Mount! The Risen Christ must have smiled at the irony that it took Christians almost two centuries to discover what he had so obviously taught about nonviolence; and not only that, but they had been led to this discovery, not by their Scripture scholars, but by a man who was not a Christian. Gandhi is supposed to have said on one occasion, with a bit of exaggeration perhaps, but surely not without a touch of humor, that the only people who do not know that Jesus taught nonviolence are Christians.

Merton and Gandhi

As I have mentioned in Chapter One, Merton's interest in Gandhi goes back to his teenage years at Oakham School in England. That interest resurfaced in the monastery. As early as 1956 his reading notebooks were filled with notes on Gandhi's understanding of nonviolence. In 1964 Merton wrote for *Ramparts* magazine an article entitled "Gandhi:

The Gentle Revolutionary." The next year he published in *Jubilee* an article entitled "Gandhi and the One-Eyed Giant," which became the introduction to a book of selections from Gandhi published that same year.

Nonviolence Calls for Total Commitment

What did Merton mean by nonviolence? First of all, it is an all-or-nothing reality. It embraces all of one's life and all of the responsibilities flowing from one's particular way of life. By that I mean I cannot choose the areas of life in which I will be nonviolent and allow myself to act violently in other situations. I cannot act nonviolently toward some people and violently toward others. I cannot decide that I shall use nonviolence when it works and jettison it when it does not. Nonviolence engages the whole person and in every situation. There is no escape from it.

It should be clear that this way of living and acting is not something I can acquire overnight. It takes time, maybe a lifetime, maybe even longer. But those who choose to commit themselves to it must be willing to struggle not only against the violence that exists in society and societal structures, but also against the hidden aggressions in themselves. This is to say that nonviolence calls for that purity of heart described in the writings of the early Fathers of the Church as the goal of spirituality. Purity of heart meant to them "an unconditional and totally humble surrender to God, a total acceptance of ourselves and our situation as willed by God" (*Contemplative Prayer*, p. 83). Purity of heart is the "climate" of nonviolence.

"Total acceptance of our situation as willed by God" does not mean acceptance of violence. *Wherever it exists violence must be resisted. This is a cardinal principle of nonviolence.* A nonviolent person can never be passive in the face of violence. Passivity is cowardice: It may in fact be a cloak that covers a good bit of hatred and inner violence that one is afraid to express. Such passivity is unworthy of a human person. To such false nonviolence Gandhi says he would prefer an honest resort to force. At least one who has recourse to force realizes that violence always has to be resisted. But Gandhi and Martin Luther King, Jr., and Thomas Merton would insist: There is a better—and ultimately more effective—way to resist evil and that is the way of nonviolence.

Nonviolence and Contemplation

The vision that motivates the nonviolent person is the contemplative vision that in God we are all one. Nonviolence cannot be built on a presupposed division between them and us. It looks rather to the fundamental unity whereby all God's creatures are united with one another. "[Nonviolence] is not out for the conversion of the wicked to the ideas of the good, but for the healing and reconciliation of man with himself, man the person and man the human family" (*Passion for Peace*, p. 249).

Commitment to the Truth

The fundamental commitment of nonviolence, therefore, is to the truth. But it is so easy for me to fall into the trap of assuming that I have all the truth. I need to be clear that the truth I am fighting for is not my truth, but the truth that is grounded in the Ultimate Reality and therefore is true for everyone. The test of our sincerity, Merton points out, is this: Are we willing to learn something from the adversary? If a new truth is made known to us through him or her, will we accept it? I recall recently having a discussion (argument?) with someone over a rather insignificant matter (whether or not one had to cross a certain interstate highway to get to a particular religious house that I had to go to the next day). Thinking about this discussion afterwards, I wondered if in the heat of it both of us had not become more interested in "being right" than in finding the truth. This, of course, was no big deal, and we were able to laugh about the heatedness of our disagreement when we met again. But it reveals how easily the need we have "to be right" can become a self-righteousness, an arrogance, that prevents us from seeing that an adversary can sometimes enlighten us in a totally unexpected way.

Respect for the Dignity of the Human Person

Thus it is that nonviolence refuses to see the oppressor as a nonperson. It sets out therefore to liberate not only the oppressed but also the oppressor whose violence prevents her or him from being free. Nonviolence, therefore desires the true good of the oppressor. For the person of nonviolence has the contemplative vision that there is a level of consciousness where oppressor and oppressed are one. This is what Jesus meant by love of enemies. Gandhi wrote: "Jesus lived and died in vain if he did not teach us to regulate the whole of life by the eternal law of love" (*Gandhi on Non-violence*, p. 26). Note how Gandhi speaks not only of Jesus' death, but also of his life as teaching the law of love. Nonviolence for Gandhi is "a complete way of life, in which the satyagrahi is totally dedicated to the transformation of his own life, of his adversary, and of society by means of love" [Ibid., p. 35]).

Nonviolence and Society

Active nonviolence must unmask the contradiction of a society that is based on force. Unfortunately, the affluent industrial society, with all the freedom it presumes to offer its people, is a society that survives because it lives by systematic greed and a subtle violence that makes the affluent richer and the nonaffluent poorer. Those who practice nonviolence will almost of necessity find themselves at odds with such a society. At the same time they must beware lest their own values be subtly subverted by the disvalues so easily disseminated by a society dedicated to profit and motivated by greed. It was no accident that Merton continually urged followers of nonviolence to guard against the violence and the aggressiveness so easily hidden undetected in their own persons. It is so easy to forget that every time I demean another person, put someone down with the cruel, cutting word, broadcast another person's faults, I am being a violent person. I am denying the gospel call to love. I am forgetting the contemplative oneness that links me to brother and sister, to friend and enemy. And every time I let go of my aggressiveness and pettiness and act in genuine unconditional love, I am releasing a wonderful healing, purifying, unifying power that can bring peace and harmony to my own life and to the lives of those with whom I live and work.

As we approach a new millennium, nonviolence is coming of age. A recent issue of *Fellowship* (July-August 1996) carried an article entitled "The Global Spread of Active Nonviolence." More and more people are discovering nonviolence as "a creative, life-affirming way to resolve conflict, to overcome oppression, establish justice, protect the earth and build democracy." One of the great challenges of the new century that will soon be upon us is to give nonviolence a chance!

∼∼∼∼∼∼∼∼∼∼∼ *8. Zen* ∼∼∼∼∼∼∼∼∼∼∼

What Zen communicates is an awareness that is potentially already there but is not conscious of itself. Zen is then not Kerygma but realization, not revelation but consciousness.... (Zen and the Birds of Appetite, *p. 47*)

"Zen teaches nothing; it merely enables us to wake up and become aware. It does not teach, it points." (D. T. Suzuki, quoted in Ibid., pp. 49-50)

One of the striking features of the last decade of Merton's life—this takes us into a whole new room in the gallery of Merton themes—was his enthusiastic interest in Asian religions, especially in Zen. Three decades earlier, in the late thirties, he had dabbled in oriental texts, only to be baffled by them. The rather sweeping conclusion he drew, writing later in *The Seven Storey Mountain*, was that oriental mysticism, while not "evil, *per se*...[was] simply more or less useless"

(p. 188). During the forties and fifties he was somewhat embarrassed by the narrowness and total misunderstanding expressed in these words. Steeping himself in the mystical tradition of the west, he came to realize *the importance of experience over verbal formulations*. The dawning of this realization enabled him to appreciate the writings of one of the foremost contemporary figures in Zen, D. T. Suzuki.

What exactly is Zen? As Merton suggests in *Mystics and Zen Masters*, "this is a dangerously loaded question" (p. 12). "Zen" comes from the Chinese word *Ch'an*, which means meditation. Yet it would be wrong to consider it simply as a method of meditation. Definitely it is not meditation in the sense in which that term is often used in the West, namely, as discursive reasoning. Discursive reasoning always involves a subject (thinking) and an object (thought about). Zen would repudiate any such division of subject and object. Viewing Zen as a westerner, Merton "defines" it as "the ontological *awareness of pure being beyond subject and object*" (Ibid., p. 14). Zen masters, however, staunchly refuse to verbalize the Zen experience. Merton attempts once again to do so in the following words: Zen is "the recognition that the whole world is aware of itself in me and that 'I' am no longer my individual and limited self...but that my 'identity' is to be sought not in that *separation* from all that is, but in oneness..." (*Mystics and Zen Masters*, pp. 17-18).

It is worth pointing out that many of the statements Merton makes about contemplation (particularly in *New Seeds of Contemplation*) could be used to describe the Zen experience. Thus, in the very first page of that book, he writes: Contemplation is "life itself, fully awake, fully aware, fully active, fully aware that it is alive." One could easily substitute "Zen" for "contemplation" and the statement would be equally true. This brings us to the question: Can one separate Zen from Zen Buddhism? Merton's response, I believe, would be in the affirmative. Thus in *Zen and the Birds of Appetite*, he describes Zen consciousness: "a trans-cultural, trans-religious, trans-formed consciousness.... [I]t can shine through this or that system, religious or irreligious, just as light can shine through glass that is blue, or green, or red, or yellow" (p. 4). Consistently Merton compares the Zen experience with Christian contemplation.

Christian writers who have had a long and fruitful contact with Zen suggest that a "Christian Zen" or a "Zen Catholicism" is a possibility. One can be true to Christian tradition and at the same time be enriched by the Zen approach to prayer and meditation. I have a good friend, a Roman Catholic priest, who has a Zen master as his spiritual director and who regularly goes to a Zen center to practice *zazen. Zazen* means sitting in meditation, striving to enter into the depths of one's self, seeking to "go down" to that inmost place (that is really no place), where subject and object disappear and all is one. While Zen scholars and Christians would describe that oneness in different ways, it is the goal of the enlightenment to which both aspire.

In Japan there are Roman Catholic priests who are also Zen masters. Father William Johnston, who has taught for many years in Japan, has written a book entitled *Christian Zen*, in which he explicitly distinguishes Zen as "meditation" from Zen Buddhism as a "religion."

It is clear, I believe, that for Merton it is Zen as meditation (with all that that implies for Zen masters), not Zen Buddhism, that he looked to for enrichment of his own spiritual and monastic tradition. He was well aware that you cannot compare Christianity and Zen as religions, that is to say, you cannot compare them at the level of doctrine. "To approach the subject [of Zen] with an intellectual or theological chip on the shoulder would end only in confusion" (*Zen and the Birds of Appetite*, p. 33). For Zen is neither an intellectual approach to reality nor a theological explanation of human existence. Christianity, on the other hand, at first sight seems to be both.

Zen is realization; it is not doctrine. Christianity is revelation; and through the centuries that revelation has been formulated into an elaborate system of doctrines. Christianity is verbal; much ink has been spilled in expounding its doctrines. Zen is interested not in the verbal, but in the real.

"When I raise the hand thus," said D. T. Suzuki, "there is Zen. But when I assert I have raised the hand, Zen is no more there" (quoted in Aelred Graham, *Zen Catholicism*, p. 19). Or, as the Zen saying goes: "The finger that points to the moon is not the moon." As soon as you conceptualize an experience and try to put it into words, you objectify it and there is danger of confusing the concept or the words with the experience itself. "The whole aim of Zen," Merton tells us, "is not to make foolproof statements about experience, but to come to direct grips with reality without the mediation of logical verbalizing" (*Zen and the Birds of Appetite*, p. 37). As one Zen master put it: "However great the conceptual knowledge and understanding may be, in the face of real experience concepts are like flakes of snow fallen on a burning fire" (Abbot Zenkei Shibayama, *A Flower Does Not Talk* [Vermont: Tuttle, 1970], p. 23). Interestingly, Thomas Merton makes a similar statement in an early work (*The Ascent to Truth*). I have used this text earlier in speaking about God, but it is worth repeating here. He speaks of the concepts we have of God, such as "love," "intelligence," "power," as tiny matches which we light. "As soon as we light these small matches...the tremendous reality of God Who infinitely exceeds all concepts bears down upon us like a dark storm and blows out all their flames" (p. 106). The significant thing to note is that these words appear in a very early Merton book (*Ascent* was published in 1951), before Merton had any serious contact with Zen. It was his grasp of the Christian mystical experience that eventually enabled him to understand Zen.

While it is futile to compare Zen and Christianity at the level of doctrine—for Christianity doctrine is of great importance; for Zen it is incidental—still there is an important point of meeting for the two: the level of experience. *Zen clearly gives priority to experience; but so does Christianity, if it is properly understood.* It is true that Christianity, unlike Zen, begins with revelation. But it is a huge mistake to think of this revelation simply as doctrine. It is the self-revelation of God calling the Christian to *experience*

God in Christ through the Spirit. Granted this revelation is communicated in words and statements, and Christians have always been profoundly concerned with the exact meaning of these statements and their precise formulation. Nonetheless, Christian theologians, at least in their better moments, have always understood that no formulation can adequately embody God's self-revelation. We have to admit, however, the fact which history testifies to so clearly: namely, that obsession with correct doctrinal formulas has often made people forget that the heart of Christianity "is a *living experience* of unity with Christ which transcends all conceptual formulations" (*Zen and the Birds of Appetite*, p. 39).

This was the understanding of the apostolic Church. The *kerygma* of the early Church was not simply an announcement of certain propositions about Jesus Christ, dead and risen; it was a summons to participate in the reality of his death and rising. It was a call to taste and experience eternal life.

> [We] declare to you the eternal life that was with the Father and was revealed to us—we declare to you what we have seen and heard so that you also may have fellowship with us; and truly our fellowship is with the Father and with his Son Jesus Christ. (1 John 1:2-3)

Christianity means much more than change in behavior: It calls us to a change in consciousness. And if it is understood in this way, it involves, just as truly as Zen, an experience that is transforming: an experience that can never be adequately put into words.

It is worth noting that among the early Christian writers theology was not so much reflection on doctrine as the actual experience of the realities that doctrines attempt to express. The Greek word *theologia* was the word they used for what we today call "contemplation."

Merton came to see that "theology" might well be the real area for discovering correspondences and relationships between Christianity and Zen, if by that term we mean "theology as experienced in Christian contemplation" (that is, the Greek *theologia*), rather than the speculative theology of the manuals and textbooks. In *Zen and the Birds of Appetite*, he explores in detail such correspondences and relationships. This book gathers together a number of his articles on Zen. Merton had hoped to bring a copy of it with him to Asia as a gift for the Dalai Lama. He was prevented from doing so, since he left for Asia on October 16 and the book was not published until October 31, 1968. Five days later he would meet with the Dalai Lama. Some five weeks later a strange and unexpected death (in Bangkok, thousands of miles away from the Abbey of Gethsemani), would usher him into the Experience that transcends all experiences.

Notes

[1] These words are found in a letter to Amiya Chakravarty in the first volume of the Merton Letters, entitled *The Hidden Ground of Love*, edited by William H. Shannon (New York: Farrar Straus and Giroux, 1985), p. 115.

[2] The "just war theory" originated in pre-Christian sources (the Stoic philosophers and Cicero) and was adopted by Augustine (354-430) as a way of accommodating the teaching of the gospel with the defense of the Roman Empire. It became the heritage of medieval theology. To be just, a war had to be (1) declared by competent authority, (2) waged for a just cause, (3) with the right intention (righting a wrong inflicted), (4) with proportionate means (including no direct attacks against innocent noncombatants) and (5) with reasonable hope for success. The advent of nuclear weapons and even of conventional weapons with terrible capabilities of destruction has led more and more people today to question the very possibility of a just war. ❦

CHAPTER FOUR

The Merton Library: What to Read First

The work of writing can be for me very close to the simple joy of being: by creative reflection and awareness to help life itself live in me. For me to write is love; it is to inquire and to praise, or to confess or to appeal.... Not to assure myself that I am ("I write, therefore I am"), but simply to pay my debt to life, to the world, to other men [and women]. To speak out with an open heart and say what seems to me to have meaning. (Unpublished Notebook CI, 1966, Syracuse University Library)

The bad writing I have done has all been authoritarian, the declaration of musts and the announcement of punishments. Bad because it implies a lack of love, good insofar as there may yet have been some love in it. The best stuff has been straight confession and witness. (Ibid.)

The work I feel more happy about is at once more personal, more literary, more contemplative. Books like *Conjectures, New Seeds, Sign of Jonas, Raids,* or literary essays or poetry, or things like introductions to Chuang Tzu, Gandhi, Desert Fathers.... The "Notes on a Philosophy of Solitude" in *Disputed Questions* is very central. (Letter to June Yungblut, March 6, 1968 in *The Hidden Ground of Love*, pp. 641-642)

As for writing: I don't feel that I can in conscience, at a time like this, go on writing just about things like meditation, though that has its point. I cannot just bury my head in a lot of rather tiny and secondary monastic studies either. I think I have to face the big issues, the life-and-death issues:

and this is what everyone is afraid of. (Letter to Dorothy Day, August 23, 1961, Ibid., p. 140)

In 1963 Merton received from the book editor of the *San Francisco Examiner* an invitation to respond to a questionnaire about books and reading. The list Merton gave of the books he was reading or that had influenced him was, I feel sure, quite different from the lists of most of the other respondents. Not many would have on their list the *Proslogion* of Saint Anselm or the sermons of Meister Eckhart, the poetic work of William Blake or the plays of Aeschylus and Sophocles. Commenting, as he had been asked to do, on the books that influenced him, Merton wrote: "These books and others like them have helped me to discover the real meaning of my life, and have made it possible for me to get out of the confusion and meaninglessness of an existence completely immersed in the needs and passivities fostered by a culture in which sales are everything" (*Witness to Freedom*, p. 166).

To discover the real meaning of human life and to be able to evade the shallowness of a culture that seems to foster accumulation of goods as life's most important purpose— these seem to me to be valuable goals to set for our lives, if we want to live as whole persons and in the real world. It is my conviction that, just as his reading helped him in moving toward these goals, so our reading of Merton's works can do the same for us.

In the previous chapter I have tried to present some of the dominant themes in Merton's works. In this chapter I want to deal with those works from which these important themes emerged. I am calling this chapter "The Merton Library." When I chose that title, I checked the word "library" in the Oxford English Dictionary, where I found a number of meanings. The word can designate "a building containing a large collection of books," or it may refer to "the large collection of books" housed in such a building. The latter meaning is not uncommon. People frequently speak of "my library," referring not so much to a special room in their home, but to their collection of books. This is the meaning I intend here.

The Intent of This Chapter

Before evaluating Merton's books, it will be helpful for us to know what Merton thought of his own books and which were his favorites. This I hope to follow with a discussion of what I consider his most important books, together with a suggested order in which one might most profitably read the books in the Merton Library.

Merton's Opinion of His Own Books

On several occasions Merton offered either a classification or an evaluation of his writings. In a letter of June 17, 1968 (to Sister John Marie, in *School of Charity*, pp. 384-85), he divides his books into three periods: (1) from his conversion in 1938 (November 16) to his ordination in 1949 (May 26), (2) from 1949 to 1960 (the year *Disputed Questions* was published), and (3) from 1960 on.

Merton's Classification

Period One: November 16, 1938, to May 26, 1949

Thirty Poems (1944)

A Man in the Divided Sea (1946)

The Seven Storey Mountain (1948)

Seeds of Contemplation (1949)

The Secular Journal (published in 1959, but actually a pre-Gethsemani journal)

Period Two: 1949 to 1960

The Sign of Jonas (1953)

No Man Is An Island (1955)

The Strange Islands (1957)

The Silent Life (1957)

Thoughts in Solitude (1959, but written for the most part in 1953)

Disputed Questions (1960, a kind of transition to the third period)

Period Three: 1960 on

Emblems of a Season of Fury (1963)

Seeds of Destruction (1964)

Gandhi on Non-Violence (1965)

The Way of Chuang Tzu (1965)

Raids on the Unspeakable (1966)

Conjectures of a Guilty Bystander (1966), etc.[1]

Writing in 1968 Merton describes the *first period* as one in which his writing was unworldly, ascetic, "first fervor" stuff. It was a time when life at Gethsemani was very strict and Merton, the fervent monk, bought it all. "Most people," Merton tells Sister John Marie, "judge me entirely by this period, either favorably or unfavorably, and do not realize that I have changed a great deal."

During the *second period* he began, as he put it, "to open up again to the world." He was reading about psychoanalysis, Zen Buddhism, existentialism as well as much more literature.

"But the fruits of this," he tells us, "did not really begin to appear until the *third period*." Indeed, he says (and remember he was writing in the last year of his life), "I am now evolving further, with studies on Zen and a new kind of experimental creative drive in prose poetry, satire, etc."

In this same letter he discusses how the changes in his

writing affected his readers: "[T]here is always a solid phalanx of people who seem to get a lot out of the early books up to about *Thoughts in Solitude*, and have never heard of the others. These tend to be people interested in the spiritual life and somewhat conservative in many ways." The result, he feels, is that there are two Mertons: one ascetic, conservative, traditional and monastic; the other, radical, independent and somewhat akin to beats and hippies and poets. He suggests that neither one of them appealed to "the current pacesetters for Catholic thought and life in the U.S. today." I believe he may well have been correct in thinking that his popularity had waned somewhat in the late sixties. But in 1978, the tenth anniversary of his death, interest in his writings experienced a strong revival. The following years saw that revival intensified; and it shows no signs of abating. Quite the contrary.

Merton's Graph of His Own Writings

In 1967 Merton did a graph (see page 130) evaluating his books. Apparently he did such a graph on two different occasions, for there are two classifications whose titles are slightly different, though they have the same basic meaning. The following are the categories he listed: best, better, good, less good (or fair), poor, very poor (or bad), awful.

Merton's Evaluation

Best

None listed.

Better

Thirty Poems

The Seven Storey Mountain

Seeds of Contemplation

Tears of the Blind Lions

Sign of Jonas

Silent Life

Thoughts in Solitude

Wisdom of the Desert

New Seeds of Contemplation

Seeds of Destruction

The Way of Chuang Tzu

Emblems of a Season of Fury

Raids on the Unspeakable

Conjectures of a Guilty Bystander

Good

A Man in the Divided Sea

No Man Is An Island

The Strange Islands

The New Man

Disputed Questions

Mystics and Zen Masters

Fair

Figures For an Apocalypse

Waters of Siloe

Ascent to Truth

Bread in the Wilderness

Last of the Fathers

Life and Holiness

Poor

Living Bread

Spiritual Direction and Meditation

Seasons of Celebration

Bad (or Very Poor)

Exile Ends in Glory

Awful

What Are These Wounds

.

Merton's Graph

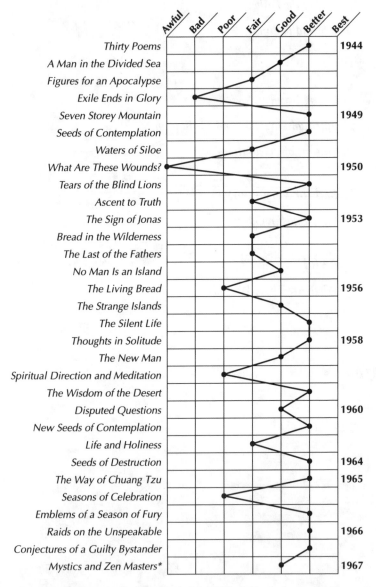

Axis labels: Awful, Bad, Poor, Fair, Good, Better, Best

Title	Rating	Year
Thirty Poems	Better	1944
A Man in the Divided Sea	Good	
Figures for an Apocalypse	Poor	
Exile Ends in Glory	Awful	
Seven Storey Mountain	Better	1949
Seeds of Contemplation	Better	
Waters of Siloe	Fair	
What Are These Wounds?	Awful	1950
Tears of the Blind Lions	Better	
Ascent to Truth	Fair	
The Sign of Jonas	Better	1953
Bread in the Wilderness	Fair	
The Last of the Fathers	Fair	
No Man Is an Island	Good	
The Living Bread	Poor	1956
The Strange Islands	Good	
The Silent Life	Better	
Thoughts in Solitude	Better	1958
The New Man	Good	
Spiritual Direction and Meditation	Poor	
The Wisdom of the Desert	Better	
Disputed Questions	Good	1960
New Seeds of Contemplation	Better	
Life and Holiness	Fair	
Seeds of Destruction	Better	1964
The Way of Chuang Tzu	Better	1965
Seasons of Celebration	Poor	
Emblems of a Season of Fury	Better	
Raids on the Unspeakable	Better	1966
Conjectures of a Guilty Bystander	Better	
Mystics and Zen Masters*	Good	1967

*Not included: *New Seeds of Contemplation* (1962), *Cables to the Ace* (1968), *Faith and Violence* (1968), *Zen and the Birds of Appetite* (1968) and some shorter works.

The reproduction of Merton's graph on page 130 classifies thirty-one of his books. It does not include a few smaller works or the three published in 1968. Neither does it embrace the (to date) twenty-seven books (including the five volumes of his letters and the first four volumes of his journals) that would be published posthumously. At this writing there are three more journals to be published. On this count thirty-one books plus were published during his lifetime and an additional thirty-two posthumously. Surely a staggering output for a monk who had but a few hours a day in which to write.

I don't want to overwhelm you with various evaluations that Merton made of his own writings. But there is a remarkable passage in one of his reading journals (under the date of December 18, 1965), in which he comments on a sentence from Rainer Maria Rilke. Rilke wrote: "A work of art is good only if it has sprung from necessity." Merton comments: "Applying this to my own books—whether they are works of art or not—I would say the following came from a kind of necessity: *Chuang Tzu, Guilty Bystander*, some of the poems in *Emblems*, "Philosophy of Solitude" [an essay in *Disputed Questions*], *Sign of Jonas, Seven Storey Mountain, Thirty Poems*. And that's about it. The rest is trash. Or rather the rest is journalism. I would say the writing on Zen was 'necessary' too. And some of *Behavior of Titans*."

In 1968 James Thomas Baker completed at Florida State University one of the earliest of many dissertations that would be written on Merton and his writings. Merton read the dissertation with interest. It was useful to him, he told Baker in a letter of June 11, 1968, to see an evaluation of his work as a whole. "It gives me some perspective on it," he said, "and I suppose the thing that strikes me most is that I have said so much that was premature, provisional, and in many ways inadequate. I am surprised that people have received these ideas, on the whole, with more respect than they deserved. I have certainly had unfriendly critics, but on the whole my work has been accepted with sympathy" (*The Hidden Ground of Love*, p. 69).

In this same letter he makes the interesting point that he felt that Catholic readers had been either too critical or too uncritical of him and that he appreciated the more objective and balanced view of his work that is sometimes taken by people outside the Catholic Church. The impression he had that he seemed to receive "either total adulation or total rejection" from his co-religionists was probably a reasonably fair assessment at the time he wrote. The two "Mertons"—the contemplative monk who wrote so splendidly about prayer and the inner life, and the social and literary critic, who had taken another and more compassionate look at the world he thought he had left—had not yet come together in many people's minds in 1968. At the present time (in the last years of the twentieth century) this dualistic perception of Merton, while still persisting in the minds of some, has to a great extent been overcome. Merton scholarship has helped us to see that contemplation and compassion, far from being incompatible with one another, are intimately and indeed necessarily linked.

One further point I should add from the letter to Baker. Merton comments on what he had written: "I must admit I really wish I had never written most of it." He made a similar comment about his works in the letter to Sister John Marie, to which I have previously referred: "Looking back on my work, I wish I had never bothered to write about one-third of it—the books that tend to be 'popular' religion. Or 'inspirational.'" These two letters were written just eight days apart. Clearly the feeling that he had written too much was on his mind at that time in 1968.

Would Merton's writings have been of better quality if he had written less and more carefully? It is a question difficult to answer. Evelyn Waugh, who pronounced favorably on *The Seven Storey Mountain* (and indeed edited its British edition under the title *Elected Silence*), still suggested to Merton that his writing would profit from greater precision and more rigorous discipline. In fact, he sent Merton a copy of Fowler's *Modern English Usage* to assist him in cleaning up his prose style. I suppose there is a point to Waugh's criticism:

Merton's writing is at times undisciplined, redundant, repetitious, "scatter bombing," as Waugh put it, rather than "precision bombing." Yet we must remember that his writing time was severely limited by the monastic schedule. More than that, the question has to be raised: Had he followed Waugh's advice and made a conscientious effort to improve his style, would his writing have lost the spontaneity, the passion, the enthusiasm that makes so much of it so appealing? Michael Mott has made the interesting point that *Elected Silence* "is a different book [from *The Seven Storey Mountain*], and it lacks the flavor of the original. A few important sections are no longer in Merton's voice" (*The Seven Mountains of Thomas Merton* [Boston: Houghton Mifflin, 1984], p. 248). I might make a final point: It seems to me that, without any conscious effort to do so, Merton did improve his writing style simply by continuing to write. He was, I believe, one of those writers whose writing improved as and because he kept at it.

1. *The Seven Storey Mountain*

Speaking of *The Seven Storey Mountain* leads immediately into the answer to the question that surely is the first to come to mind in approaching Merton's books: Where should one start? There can be no doubt that *The Seven Storey Mountain* is the place. It is the book that has drawn hundreds of thousands of people—of different backgrounds, religions, languages, races, countries, continents—to Thomas Merton. Without exaggeration, it may well be called the greatest and most influential spiritual book of the twentieth century. It has given direction to the spirituality of countless men and women who, whether they have any institutional religious ties or not, have found in *The Mountain* a beacon drawing them to a life deeper than any they had ever known before.

If it can be said that Merton was a born writer, one might almost say that *The Seven Storey Mountain* was the book he was born to write. It was a book in process of being formed inside of him for a long time until it finally burst out. He had written novels since he was a school boy in France. An interesting bit of information about his childhood writing appears in a letter of September 12, 1959, to John Harris, at the time a teacher in Devonshire, England. Merton writes:

> When you wrote from Exeter I remember a strange time in France, when I had a passionate desire to see Exeter and wrote a novel about it. Why, God only knows. I was fourteen[2] and the novel was a kind of mixture of *Westward Ho* and *Lorna Doone*. (*The Hidden Ground of Love*, p. 394)

He also wrote several novels while he was a student at Columbia. But none of them found a publisher. Robert Giroux, a young editor at Harcourt Brace, rejected them. His comment on one of them: "Merton has writing ability, but this wobbles around, and gets nowhere" (*Merton by Those Who Knew Him Best*, p. 17). What he had been unable to do in these abortive attempts, he finally accomplished in *The Mountain*: He produced a narrative that "got somewhere." It got somewhere, because, when he wrote it, his life had begun to go somewhere.

A Best-Seller

Published in 1948, it became an instant best-seller. It launched him into the literary "big leagues." Such celebrity-status brought the assurance that whatever else he was to write would receive serious attention. He was a writer to be reckoned with. The book was widely and very favorably reviewed. Edward Barry in the *Chicago Tribune* describes it as "of intense interest and timeless value. Engrossing from first page to last." Ann F. Wolfe, writing for the *Saturday Review of Literature*, saw it as "essentially the odyssey of a soul. As such it stands as a more human document than the comparable *Apologia Pro Vita Sua* of John Henry Newman. It has warmth and gusto and Augustinian wit." Msgr. (later Bishop) Fulton J. Sheen described it as "a Twentieth Century form of the *Confessions* of St. Augustine." James O. Supple in his review in the *Chicago Sun Times* expressed as well as anyone the reason for its appeal. He calls it "a hymn of positive faith sung in the midst of a purposeless world searching for purpose. A book that can be read with fascination by the man of any faith or none at all." In the same vein, Graham Greene writes: "It is a rare pleasure to read an autobiography with a pattern and meaning valid for all of us. *The Seven Storey Mountain* is a book one reads with a pencil so as to make it one's own." Clare Boothe Luce indulged in a bit of prophecy: "It is to a book like this that men will turn a hundred years from now to find out what went on in the heart of man in this cruel century."

Merton wrote a large number of books after *The Seven Storey Mountain*, yet it still remains true that to understand his later works, one has to know the Merton of *The Mountain*. I agree with the view expressed by Elena Malits that "the book is embryonic: all the essential structural components of Merton's later works are there, though many in undeveloped form" (*Spiritual Life*, 27 [summer 1981, p. 74]). *The Mountain* is the door that leads into the rest of the Merton Library.

~.~ *Perennial Interest in* The Seven Storey Mountain ~.~

The amazing fact about *The Mountain* is that it has remained a "best-seller" or, perhaps I should put it more modestly, it simply keeps on selling and selling and selling,[3] and in an increasing number of languages, both western and eastern. This is especially amazing as the book unmistakably reflects the Catholicism of the 1940's—not a particularly fertile or creative period in the Church's life, especially when compared to the Catholicism that erupted a couple of decades later as the fruit of the Second Vatican Council. *The Seven Storey Mountain* in 1948 may have appealed to some readers because it presented Catholic thought of the 1940's: the belief that in the things of God Catholics were right and Protestants wrong. Catholics were on the true road to salvation; Protestants and others could be saved only because of their invincible ignorance. Catholics went to Church to please God or at least to fulfill a religious obligation; Protestants went to show off their Sunday clothes. No wonder that a later Merton was embarrassed by the narrowness and smugness of his "best-seller." To a correspondent he wrote on January 10, 1964: "[A] lot of water has gone under the bridge in the years (almost twenty) since I wrote *The Seven Storey Mountain*. I would have said many things differently today..." (*Witness to Freedom*, p. 310). To an Anglican woman disturbed about remarks he had made about Anglicanism, he wrote, on April 2, 1965: "Your supposition that if I wrote that book again today I would speak differently of Anglicans was both charitable and correct. My thought at the time of writing was hardly matured.... It is, unfortunately, so easy and so usual simply to compare the dark side of someone else's Church with the bright side of one's own. Thank heaven, we are getting over that now, I hope" (Ibid., p. 319). To a high school student in California who wrote in July of 1967 asking what he would do if he had to rewrite *The Seven Storey Mountain*, he wrote: "I'd cut out a lot of the sermons, I guess, including the sales pitch for Catholic schools and that" (*The Road to Joy*, p. 310).

Ongoing Appeal

How does a book, seemingly so dated, continue to appeal to readers now, nearly fifty years after it was first published? The only way I can explain it is that the magnanimity of the author, his sincerity and genuineness, somehow transcend the shortcomings of his theology. Moreover, the book is full of very vivid narratives that overshadow the pious reflections that at times becloud its pages. Finally, there are in his story perennial elements of human experience and concern that parallel the human journey of every man and every woman. This book is a profoundly human story.

How to Approach The Seven Storey Mountain

Yet one does have to face the fact that *The Seven Storey*

Mountain was published nearly fifty years ago. How should a prospective reader approach it today? Read it, I would suggest, to share the story of a man who became a pilgrim in search of life's meaning. About one-quarter of the way through *The Seven Storey Mountain*, Thomas Merton, an eighteen-year-old tourist come to Rome to have a good time, unaccountably found himself drawn to churches and basilicas. "And thus," he writes, "without knowing anything about it, I became a pilgrim" (p. 108).

Many of us, as we draw close to the beginning of a new century, can identify with this pilgrim role and the need to search for life's deepest meanings. So many of the old certainties that we once took for granted are up for grabs. So many structures that we had placed our faith in seem to be crumbling about us. We may not be comfortable with where we are. That is why many today face the choice either to live with life's apparent meaninglessness or to get on with the search. That is why Merton's story, though lived out in different times and under different circumstances, may interlock with our stories and give us the courage and the insight to continue along a path that seems at times flooded with a light that beckons and at other times shadowed by a darkness that threatens. Like Merton, we have become pilgrims: searchers for a source of truth and goodness. We seek a life that has significance beyond the superficial and the temporal, a life that leads us into the very heart of God.

Will *The Seven Storey Mountain* answer all our questions? Of course not. It will, however, help us to begin to sort out what are the really important questions and enable us to see what the issues are that really matter. After all, *The Seven Storey Mountain* is the door to the Merton Library. Once we get inside, we will come to realize that Merton grew far beyond what he was able to write in *The Mountain*. As we move about in the Library, we can see his growth, can accompany him on his journey and perhaps be charmed into growing with him. ✦

Merton's title is taken from the poet Dante Alighieri who, in
the second part of his *Divine Comedy*, the *Purgatorio*, narrates
the human journey in terms of a climb up the seven tiers of
purgatory. I say "the human journey," because, as Alan Jones
has pointed out in his excellent book, *The Soul's Journey*, this
great medieval classic is not Dante's story; it is everyman's
and everywoman's. Inferno, Purgatorio, Paradiso are not
places but experiences that enter into every human life. They
are, Jones points out, part of everyone's journey "from the
hell of attachment to the heaven of consciousness" (p. 29).
The defining metaphor, he believes, is love, *eros*, understood
as the deep longings and desires that fill the human heart.
The theme of Dante's poem, Jones suggests, is the purifying
of these desires. We have to learn what is worthy of our
desiring. This means that our desiring will never come to an
end except in God who is no end. Dante knew well
Augustine's oft-quoted words: "Our hearts are restless till
they find their rest in You." In the concluding lines of part
three of the *Divine Comedy*, the *Paradiso*, the poet finds that
rest in "the Love that moves the sun and all the stars."

Merton chose to take his title from the Purgatorio,
because his story is the narrative of the journey leading to the
purification of his own desires, a journey that culminates in
his deep desire for God. Near the end of *The Seven Storey
Mountain*, he writes: "[My God, I desire]...to be lost to all
created things, to die to them and to the knowledge of them,
for...I [know] that it is only by leaving them that I [can] come
to You" (p. 421). His coming to God is what *The Seven Storey
Mountain* is all about: that arduous, upward, seven-tiered
journey that leads to the threshold of paradise.

～～～～～ *The Pilgrim's Journey Continues* ～～～～～

This is not to say that Merton's spiritual journey ends with
the final pages of his autobiography. The rest of his books
continue the story of this pilgrim of the Absolute. As he

wrote, near the end of *The Seven Storey Mountain*:

> In one sense we are always travelling, and travelling as if we did not know where we were going. In another sense we have already arrived. We cannot arrive at the perfect possession of God in this life, and that is why we are travelling and in darkness. But we already possess Him by grace, and therefore in that sense we have arrived and are dwelling in the light.
>
> But oh! How far I have to go to find you in Whom I have already arrived (p. 419).

References to Dante

Twice in *The Mountain* Merton mentions Dante. On pages 122 and 123 he recalls that the one grace he got from being in Cambridge in 1934 was that winter term's study of Dante with Professor Bullough: "In the winter term we had begun with the *Inferno*, and had progressed slowly.... And now Dante and Virgil had come through the icy heart of hell...and had climbed out to the peaceful sea at the foot of *the seven-circled mountain* of Purgatory" (p. 122). The other reference is more personal, as he related it to the time of his baptism into the Catholic Church on November 16, 1938. He writes: "I was about to set foot on the shore at the foot of the high, seven-circled mountain of Purgatory steeper and more arduous than I was able to imagine, and I was not at all aware of the climbing I was about to have to do. The essential thing was to begin the climb" (p. 221).

Suggestions for Reading The Seven Storey Mountain

It is not my intent to tell the story of *The Seven Storey Mountain*, apart from what I have said earlier about his life's story. I would like to offer some suggestions that might make the reading of this book more profitable and enjoyable.

First of all, one needs to remember that this is a spiritual autobiography, with a focus on conversion, grace and spirituality.

Second, a reader should keep in mind that this book was written by a monk, looking back over his life and viewing that life through a monastic lens. It is almost as if a monk is telling the story of someone other than himself: Brother Louis describing the youthful years of a young man named Thomas Merton and judging this worldly-minded intellectual, this lonely wanderer, from the perspective of the serenity and solitude he had come to experience in the monastery. This means that the text of *The Seven Storey Mountain* carries three different levels of meaning: (a) the historical level—what actually happened, (b) the recollected level—how Merton remembered what happened, and (c) the interpretative level—the meaning that Merton the monk gave to the remembered past.

Third, I want to point out some things that might be missed in reading, namely, the quotation on the title page (which is intended to tell us something about the book as a whole) and the chapter titles (which help us to understand the different parts of the book).

The Title Page

The title page carries a quotation from Luke's Gospel (3:8): "For I tell you that God is able of these stones to raise up children to Abraham." The intent of this epigraph is to show the power of God's grace working in the life of this writer. Grace can touch the most hardened of hearts and soften them with its caress. Merton's conversion is the story of God's grace doing just that to a heart that had become, so he thought, as hard as stone. Grace brooks no obstacle, however huge. Merton's story can be read as his "confessions," but with a meaning akin to Saint Augustine's use of that word: namely, confessing and praising God for God's gracious goodness in bringing a sinner to repentance and new life. As I have already mentioned, Fulton J. Sheen saw the kinship of *The Seven Storey Mountain* with Augustine's *Confessions*.

Structurally, *The Seven Storey Mountain* has three parts: the first and third parts with four chapters each, the second part with two chapters. And there is an epilogue.

Let us now examine each part.

Part One

Part One, pages 3 through 165, covers Merton's life from his birth (1915) to the death of his grandmother (1937). There are four chapters:

1. *Prisoner's Base.* Merton likens his earliest years to a game he played as a child. In this child's game two teams try to capture opposing players by tagging them. Those tagged are brought to a "base" where they are required to stay as prisoners. In the second sentence of his autobiography Merton describes himself as "the *prisoner* of my own violence and my own selfishness." This may be the way in which he intends this analogy to be understood: that he put himself in the prisoner's "base." But analogies may have more than one meaning. He may have been referring to the times he was "tagged" and brought to places not of his own choosing. This would include traveling with his father to, among other places, Bermuda and France. This chapter concludes with his father's announcement that he is taking Tom to France. He writes: "[O]n August the twenty-fifth of that year [1925] the game of Prisoner's Base began again, and we sailed for France" (p. 29).

2. *Our Lady of the Museums.* Beginning on page 30, this second chapter covers the years in France and the arrival in England in 1929. The title "Our Lady of the Museums" refers, I presume, to the many churches and monasteries (many of them in ruins) which he visited, as his father trudged around the countryside looking for inspiration for his paintings.

3. *The Harrowing of Hell.* Chapter Three begins on page 68 with his entrance into Oakham School (autumn 1929) and concludes with his final departure from England (November 1934) after a disastrous year at Clare College, Cambridge. The

word "harrow" means "to rob" or "to despoil." The "harrowing of hell" refers to Christ's triumphant descent into hell (that is, the lower regions, Hades) after his crucifixion to bring back the souls of the righteous who had been held captive there since the beginning of the world. This is what we mean when we say in the creed: "He descended into hell." The reference to Merton's life is clear: Christ despoils the hell in which he was held captive and raises him up from the depths into which he had fallen.

4. *The Children in the Market.* Chapter Four starts on page 131 with his return from England (November 1934) and his entrance into Columbia University (January 1935) and ends with the death of his grandmother (August 1937). The title is from Matthew's Gospel: 11:16. Jesus is describing the reactions of the people of his time to himself and to John the Baptist. John was a man of great austerity and they said he had a demon. Jesus ate and drank with all sorts of people and they see him as a drunkard and a friend of sinners. Jesus remarks that they are like "children in the marketplaces" who are never satisfied: "We played the flute for you, and you did not dance; we wailed, and you did not mourn."

The title fits well this period of Merton's life: a time of indecision, of changing moods. He enjoyed Columbia and became involved in the life of the university; yet at the same time he experienced an inner, spiritual emptiness. At one point he says: "I had discovered in myself something of a capacity for work and for activity and for enjoyment that I had never dreamed of" (p. 153). At another point, he describes, in a tersely graphic sentence, the horrible inner anguish he was enduring: "I was bleeding to death" (p. 164).

Part Two

Part Two, pages 169 to 255, tells the Merton story from his initial interest in Catholicism to his baptism and concludes with his desire to become a priest. It covers a period of only two and a half years (from February 1937 to September 1939), but they were decisive years in this young man's life. At the center of this part is the narrative of his baptism, November 16, 1939. He was twenty-four years old. The two chapters in Part Two both have titles drawn from Scripture.

1. *With a Great Price*. The text is from Paul's first epistle to the Corinthians 6:20. Paul is telling his Corinthian disciples that their bodies are the temple of the Holy Spirit who is in them. He goes on to say: "For you were bought with a price." The phrase Merton uses adds the adjective "great," which is not found in the Greek text, but would have been in the Latin Vulgate which Merton often used and in the Rheims translation of the New Testament (the only English translation at that time approved by the Roman Catholic Church). It was the grace of God, won for us by the passion, death and resurrection of Jesus, that brought to Merton the wondrous gift of faith. He knew himself bought *at a great price*.

2. *The Waters of Contradiction*. This chapter, beginning on page 226, recounts his story from the time after his baptism to the momentous decision that he wanted to be a priest (1938 to autumn 1939). The words of the chapter title come from the book of Numbers 20:13. Again these are words from the Vulgate and from the Rheims translation. A modern translation would read as follows: "These are the waters of Meribah [rather than "contradiction"], where the people of Israel quarreled with the Lord, and by which he showed his holiness." The background of this scriptural reference is the murmuring of the Israelites in the desert: They are bitter with Moses for having brought them out of Egypt. Suddenly life in Egypt did not seem quite so bad to them. They are tempted and want to return there. This was in some ways Merton's situation after his baptism. He felt he was not doing enough to strengthen the grace of his baptism and fearful that he might be slipping back into his former ways of life. At one point he offers advice to anyone just come into the Church,

advice which he realized he must follow himself: "Whoever you are, the land to which God has brought you is not like the land of Egypt from which you came out. You can no longer live here as you lived there. Your old life and your former ways are crucified now, and you must not seek to live any more for your own gratification, but give up your own judgement into the hands of a wise director, and sacrifice your pleasures and comforts for the love of God and give the money you no longer spend on those things, to the poor" (p. 232). This chapter ends with a moment of crisis. Merton is in a church and prays: "Yes, I want to be a priest, with all my heart I want it. If it is Your will, make me a priest" (p. 255). ’

Part Three

Part Three, consisting of four chapters—pages 259 through 404—extends from September 1939, when Merton talked with Dan Walsh about becoming a priest, through his first years in the monastery to April 17, 1943, the death of his brother, John Paul.

1. *Magnetic North.* The central theme of this chapter is Merton's acceptance as a Franciscan and then his subsequent rejection by the order. "Magnetic north" is the north pole as indicated on a compass, that is, when the needle of the compass is in a vertical position. This differs from what is geographically the north pole. Hence the magnetic north is always a bit off from true north. This chapter tells of Merton's desire to be a Franciscan. He had been accepted for the novitiate, then that acceptance was withdrawn. The title "magnetic north" seems to suggest that Merton was moving in the right direction, but a little off center. He would achieve his true vocation (true north) only when he entered Gethsemani.

2. *True North.* This key chapter in Merton's story, pages 299 to 336, tells of his first year of teaching at St. Bonaventure, during which he goes to Gethsemani for Holy Week. He

prays that he may return and belong in that monastery. He discovers his "true north."

3. *The Sleeping Volcano*. Chapter Nine—pages 337 to 371— tells of a brief but most significant period in his life (September to December 1941). The longing to be a Trappist smoldering in his heart ("the sleeping volcano"), finally "erupts," as he finally asks the question he had so long feared to ask and is assured that there is no impediment to his becoming a priest. He leaves St. Bonaventure on the ninth of December, arriving at Gethsemani the following day.

4. *The Sweet Savor of Liberty*. This chapter, pages 372 to 404, describes Merton's initial years in the monastery and concludes with his poem on the death of his brother (April 17, 1943). He found in the monastic life the true freedom that up to now had always eluded him. "Brother Matthew," he writes at the beginning of the chapter, "locked the gate behind me and I was enclosed in the four walls of my new freedom" (p. 372). As time went on he would see freedom in a different light, but that we shall see later when we look at other books of his.

The Epilogue

Meditatio Pauperis in Solitudine ("Meditation in Solitude of a Man Who Is Poor"). The original manuscript of *The Seven Storey Mountain* (probably composed between 1944 and 1946) ended with the poem grieving for his brother. The Epilogue, which was added later, is made up of three blocks of material: (a) pages 407 to 414—material about the monastery, including Merton's struggle about writing (written perhaps May or June of 1947); (b) pages 414 to 419—material about contemplative orders, extracts from an article of Merton's that appeared in the December 5, 1947, issue of *Commonweal* under the title "Active and Contemplative Orders"; and (c) the final prayer which came to him as an inspiration on the feast of the Sacred Heart, 1947.

The Seven Storey Mountain was accepted for publication in January 1948. The publication date was October 4, 1948. Significantly, the very last line of the book is a veiled promise that there is more to come from this energetic monk: "*Sit finis libri, non finis quaerendi*, which means: "Let this be the end of the book, but not the end of the searching."

2. *The Sign of Jonas*

For many "veteran" Merton readers the *Sign of Jonas* is their favorite in the Merton Library. They love its intimacy and spontaneity, its enthusiastic and joyful piety. A journal, it was begun in December 1946, when he had been six years at Gethsemani. It concludes with July 1952, his eleventh year in the monastery.

It is a happy book, despite the fact that the monk who wrote it found himself struggling with serious questions, such as: Can one be a contemplative and a writer? How does one relate a growing desire for solitude to the need for community? Was he in the right monastery? Should he become a Carthusian hermit?

The book's title derives from a reference to the "sign of Jonah," which appears in Matthew 12:39-41 and Luke 11:29-32. The name "Jonas" which Merton uses is the Greek form of the name of the prophet who in Hebrew is called "Jonah." It appears in the Vulgate and in the Rheims translation, the translations Merton would have had available to him at the time. Modern translations tend to follow the Hebrew spelling, "Jonah."

~~~~~~~ The Biblical Book of Jonah ~~~~~~~

The Book of Jonah is a fictional work, probably written some time after the Babylonian exile. It carries an important lesson for God's people. The story begins with Jonah receiving a commission from God to preach to the Assyrians of Nineveh. The Assyrians, the first imperial power to plunder the

Israelites and who took the northern kingdom into exile, stand in the book of Jonah not so much as an historical nation, but as a type of people hostile to Israel.

Jonah is filled with horror at the very thought of preaching repentance to the "enemy." So, to thwart God's designs, he gets on a ship going in the opposite direction. A storm arises. Jonah is blamed and thrown overboard. But God will not be frustrated. He has a great fish swallow Jonah, who remains in the fish's belly for three days, where he sings a psalm! The fish vomits him on the shore in the direction of Nineveh. Jonah finally gets the hint, goes to Nineveh, preaches repentance, and to his dismay they listen to his preaching and are saved from destruction. Displeased with the "success" of his mission, he sulks in a booth under the shade of a gourd. The gourd is attacked by a worm and withers. Jonah is exposed to the hot sun and grieves at the destruction of the gourd. His grief at the fate of the gourd becomes a lesson for him: how much more would God grieve at having a whole city with its people and cattle destroyed. God's compassion and forgiveness are contrasted with the attitude of Jonah, typical of the Israelites—so enthralled with their own belief that they are God's chosen ones that they cannot believe that God would be, or should be, concerned about any other peoples. The book is a protest against the narrowness and exclusivism that appeared in post-exilic Judaism.

The Sign of Jonah in the Gospels

This is the background of the sign of Jonah referred to by Matthew and Luke. In both Gospels Jesus is asked for a sign to confirm that he is from God. He refuses to offer any sign except that of Jonah. For Matthew the sign is one that will come in the future: the resurrection of Jesus as being three days in the belly of the earth. For Luke the sign is the repentance of the Ninevites which authenticates the mission of Jonah. Jesus calls people to repent and hear the good news. They will understand the authenticity of his message only when they repent.

On the opening page of *The Sign of Jonas*, Merton uses the interpretations of both the Gospels. Following Matthew, he says that all followers of Christ are signed with the sign of Jonas, because we all live by the power of Christ's resurrection. Following Luke, he suggests: "I find myself traveling toward my destiny in the belly of a paradox." Like Jonas, he seems to want one thing and God (speaking through his superiors) seems to want another. Frequently at various points in this book, Merton feels that he should join a more contemplative order, such as the Carthusians or the Camaldolese; he is told by his superiors, however, that he is where he belongs, namely at the Abbey of Our Lady of Gethsemani. Threading its way through the book is his persistent appeal to his superiors to change their minds. In the end he capitulates to their decision—at least for the time. This nagging feeling that he may not be in the right place will surface again later in his life.

Structure and Contents

Structurally *The Sign of Jonas* is made up of a Prologue, six Parts and an Epilogue. Its contents consist of (a) episodes in Merton's life, oftentimes commonplace events, but brimming over with meaning for him and (b) his reflection on people (abbots, retreat masters, spiritual directors, fellow-monks), on life in the monastery, on his reading and his writings, on Scripture and liturgy, on nature and natural phenomena. This last is an especially appealing aspect of *Jonas*: His love for nature and his remarkable ability to articulate its beauty endear him to his readers, and especially those with a strong sense of ecological awareness.

Merton described the book's contents as "a collection of personal notes and meditations" (p. 3). This collection includes spontaneous jottings of fleeting moments and passing reflections. There are also carefully crafted passages, clearly written with an eye to publication.

There is a narrative level to the book, where he speaks of

the world around him: the world of nature and of the monastic life. There is also a psychological and spiritual level, which reflects his experiences and what they meant to him, his changing moods, his concern for silence and solitude in a monastery that was rapidly changing from a way of life not far removed from medieval times to one that was much more modern, and also (as Merton found to his dismay) more noisy, busy and hurried. We see also how he felt about his own writing. We share his reflection on Scripture and liturgy. He is able to open his soul to us, and so often what he says speaks what is in our own hearts. For those readers who feel an affection for Merton, reading *Jonas* is somewhat like looking at an annotated family album about the leader of the family. This sense of intimacy with the writer is a delight to experience.

For the journal does have a vivid concreteness. Merton writes of spirituality, not in abstract terms, but at the level of experience. "I have attempted," he writes in the Prologue, "to convey something of a monk's spiritual life and of his thoughts, not in the language of speculation but in terms of personal experience. This," he points out, "is always a little hazardous, because it means leaving the sure, plain path of an accepted terminology and traveling in byways of poetry and intuition" (p. 8). Technical language may be universal and certain and useful for theologians, but it does not "convey what is most personal and most vital in religious experience" (p. 9). He is not speaking, therefore, of dogmas of faith, but rather of their repercussions in the life of a person in whom they are beginning to find concrete realization. The "byways of poetry and intuition" were roads much more suited to Merton's temperament than the more traveled highways of theological speculation.

~~~~~~~~~~~~ *Key Events* ~~~~~~~~~~~~

The key events of *Jonas* are his profession of perpetual and solemn vows (March 19, 1947), his ordination to the priesthood (May 26, 1949), his appointment (Trinity Sunday

1951) as Master of Scholastics (monks studying for the priesthood) and his becoming an American citizen (June 26, 1951). But what gives the book its magnetism are the many small, seemingly insignificant events that made up the daily routine of his life. Vicariously living that routine with him is what gives this book its special charm.

I should point out that, while *Jonas* still displays the buoyancy of spirit and delight in life behind the "four walls" of his newly-found freedom, there are subtle indications of the walls opening up a bit. Thus, in the entry for March 3, 1951, there is this significant statement: "Coming to the monastery has been for me exactly the right kind of withdrawal. It has given me perspective. It has taught me how to live. And now I *owe everyone else in the world a share in that life*. My first duty is to start, for the first time, to live as a member of a human race which is no more (and no less) ridiculous than I am myself. And my first human act is the recognition of how much I owe everybody else" (pp. 322-323, italics added). Is this the rebel's voice, muted for so long a time, beginning to emerge? Will his life be more and more influenced by the question: How can I share my life with those outside the monastery? Though the answer was by no means clear, Merton was more and more sure that it was the right question.

Things to Ponder

Things you might want to look for in *The Sign of Jonas*: Merton's remarks about prayer and contemplation and solitude, his reflections on the meaning of the monastic life, his comments on his own writing and reading, the many prayers that thread their way through the book, his description of nature and natural phenomena. Note especially the beauty of the Epilogue, "Fire Watch, July 4, 1952." Compare the voice of God concluding *The Sign of Jonas* with God's voice ending *The Seven Storey Mountain*. ☙

3. *No Man Is An Island*

Published in 1955, *No Man Is An Island* is probably the next book we should take off the shelves of the Merton Library. Like *The Seven Storey Mountain* and *The Sign of Jonas*, it is still in print and still being read. The title, a well-known and somewhat overworked sentence taken from John Donne, hardly captures the book's main thrust. The sense of community we all have with one another, which the title suggests, is clarified in the Prologue; and while it casts its light over the chapters of the book, it is not for all that their principal emphasis. The book is about "some of the basic verities on which the spiritual life depends" (p. 7). It is dedicated (in Latin) to the scholastics and to the newly ordained priests of the monastery of Our Lady of Gethsemani, for whom Merton had been spiritual master. One suspects that much of it emerged from lectures given to these monks. There are times when it seems clear that Merton is talking to monks. This characteristic of some of Merton's writings, especially the earlier works, can prove irritating to his readers who are not monks. It suggests an impatience on his part (or, to be more charitable, a lack of time) to do the proper editing that a careful writer needs to do.

Merton links *No Man Is an Island* with two previous works. One was a much smaller work: a mimeographed text simply called *Sentences*. This work of thirty pages is made up of some 120 sentences, some that are simply sentences; others, sentences that expand into paragraphs. On January 13, 1959, Merton sent the typescript of *Sentences* to Sister Therese Lentfoehr, telling her that it formed the rudimentary basis for *No Man Is an Island* and remarking that its short sentences were probably better than "the long-winded finished book."

Sentences was completed on the feast of the Sacred Heart 1952. *No Man Is an Island* was published March 24, 1955. This suggests that Merton would probably have completed the writing of the manuscript sometime in 1954. Thus he had about two years to transform *Sentences* into *No Man Is an*

Island. Having read *Sentences* and compared it with *No Man Is an Island*, I must say that, despite Merton's self-deprecatory statement about the book, the book is by far the better of the two works. Even though Merton mused in his letter to Sister Therese that he might some day publish *Sentences*, I would have to say that it would have required a great deal of rewriting before becoming publishable material. And *No Man Is an Island* is that rewrite.

The other link with previous writing that Merton makes is with *Seeds of Contemplation* which was published on March 2, 1949. In the Author's Note to *No Man Is an Island*, Merton indicates that it is actually a sequel to *Seeds of Contemplation*, though he makes the point that instead of going on from where that book left off, he is returning to the same material, intending to make it "simpler, more fundamental, and more detailed" (p. 7). Incidentally, this Author's Note is dated January 1955 (perhaps written after he had corrected the galleys or the page proofs?) and is signed by Fr. M. Louis, O.C.S.O., though the title page bears the name of Thomas Merton.

I doubt if many readers would find *No Man Is an Island* "simpler" than *Seeds of Contemplation*, though they might agree that it is "more detailed." Definitely, it is, in my opinion, "more fundamental." In saying this, I am understanding "fundamental" to mean "foundational." Foundational to the faith that Merton professed is "tradition" and the role it plays in giving intelligibility to that faith.

~~~~~~ The Meaning of Catholic Tradition ~~~~~~

No Man Is an Island presents a much more mature understanding of tradition than *Seeds of Contemplation*. In *Seeds of Contemplation* tradition seems to be something "out there," something of a standard against which he must measure whatever he says. Thus he writes in the Author's Note of *Seeds of Contemplation*: "We sincerely hope [this book] does not contain a line that is new to Catholic tradition" (p. 14). There is an almost disconcerting certitude threading its way through *Seeds of Contemplation*. For instance, in Chapter Twelve, which bears the title "Tradition and Revolution," Merton writes: "The reason why Catholic tradition is a tradition is because there is only one living doctrine in Christianity: there is nothing new to be discovered" (p. 84). When he calls that tradition revolutionary, he means that it opposes the values and standards of a materialistic culture. What he does not mean is that there is any revolution in the tradition itself. No, that is quite fixed. Understandably, this chapter then goes on to discuss Catholic dogma, which articulates the definitive form which that tradition takes.

No Man Is an Island, by contrast, presents a quite different understanding of Catholic tradition. This man who in 1949 did not want to write "a line that would be new to Catholic tradition," says in his 1955 book: "I do not intend to divorce myself at any point from Catholic tradition. But neither do I intend to accept points of that tradition blindly, and without understanding, and without making them really my own" (p. 11). He goes on: "For it seems to me that the first responsibility of a man of faith is to make his faith really part of his own life, not by rationalizing it [as in *Seeds of Contemplation* perhaps?] but by living it." These are the words of a man who is no longer willing to accept prepackaged answers that require no personal struggle. More than that he is willing to live with questions that for the time being may not admit of clear answers. This of course makes for a certain amount of insecurity. But the insecurity that accompanies a willingness to live with questions is preferable to "a far worse insecurity, which comes from being afraid to ask the right questions—because they might turn out to have no answer." Merton paints the dark picture of people "huddling together in the pale light of an insufficient answer to a question we are afraid to ask" (p. 10).

Such words, written more than forty years ago, have a strikingly contemporary ring when we think of some of the questions the Catholic Church struggles with today. To take but one example: There is in some quarters a hope that in the future there will be a sufficient number of celibate male priests to enable the Church to continue to be a eucharistic Church. Is this really an expression of hope or does it betray a fear of new questions and new answers? Is it, quite simply, being content with the "pale light of an insufficient answer"?

~~~~~~~~ Anticipating Vatican II ~~~~~~~~

It may be said, moreover, that Merton's perception of tradition in *No Man Is an Island* was ahead of his time. This living understanding of tradition—as growing and subject to ongoing scrutiny rather than statically fixed—anticipates the position that would be set forth ten years later in the Second Vatican Council's *Dogmatic Constitution on Divine Revelation*: "The God who spoke of old, still maintains an uninterrupted conversation with the bride of his beloved Son. The Holy Spirit, too, is active, making the living voice of the gospel ring out in the Church, and through it in the world, leading those who believe into the whole truth, and making the message of Christ dwell in them in all its richness" (art. 8).

Merton said it quite as well in Chapter Eight of *No Man Is an Island*, where he writes:

> Tradition, which is always old, is at the same time ever new because it is always reviving—born again in each new generation, *to be lived and applied in a new and particular way*.... [T]radition is *creative*. Always original, it always opens out *new horizons for an old journey*.... [It] teaches us how to live, because it develops and expands our powers, and shows us how to give ourselves to the world in which we live (pp. 120-21, italics added).

I have spent what may seem an inordinate amount of time on Merton's changing understanding of tradition. I do this for two reasons. First and foremost, because I believe that the evolution his thinking underwent on this issue tells us a great deal about Thomas Merton. It reveals a new and more mature Merton: a man whose horizons are wider, whose vision of reality is clearer, and whose perspective on life is more balanced. Understanding this change in him is crucial for forecasting the direction his life and works would take in the years that remained. For this reason *No Man Is an Island* must be seen as a key book in the Merton corpus.

I have a second reason for dwelling on a single issue. The author has chosen a literary genre which is difficult to review with any sense of completeness. Sixteen topics are discussed. All are related to the life of the spirit, but the author makes little effort to relate them to one another. A hapless reviewer who tries to give a brief introduction to this book to help readers get into it finds himself or herself with sixteen small "books" to review. The easiest way out is to excerpt quotes from a book in which so much is quotable. The text has a lyric quality. It abounds in aphorisms, clear, succinct and challenging. A few examples will suffice. "May God preserve me from the love of a friend who will never dare to rebuke me. May He preserve me from the friend who seeks to do nothing but change and correct me" (p. 10). "Renunciation is not an end in itself; it helps us to use things better" (p. 34). "The real purpose of asceticism is to disclose the difference between the evil use of created things, which is sin, and their good use, which is virtue" (p. 106). "There is something in the depths of our being that hungers for wholeness and finality" (p. 140). A favorite of mine, touching as it does on the roots of nonviolence, is this gem: "A man of sincerity is less interested in defending the truth than in stating it clearly, for he thinks that if truth be clearly seen it can very well take care of itself" (p. 195). And this: "The God of peace is never glorified by human violence" (p. 197).

The temptation is to go on quoting passage after passage. At the same time, it must be said that some of the aphorisms, so beautifully articulated, cry out for further clarification. The genre in which Merton has chosen to write gives him dispensation from this responsibility and at times leaves the reader cliff-hanging. Furthermore, there are times when one wonders if he sometimes sacrifices clarity to cleverness— surely no small temptation for a writer whose love for words and whose intuition of the power they could wield are so obvious.

When Merton made the 1967 chart rating his books, he classified *No Man Is an Island* as "GOOD." My inclination is to disagree with him and move it up one notch to "BETTER." It has survived several decades. I predict it will survive many more.

4. *New Seeds of Contemplation*

On July 1, 1948, Merton finished the writing of a book to which he gave the title *Seeds of Contemplation*. It was completed, therefore, before the publication and phenomenal success that were to mark the publication of *The Seven Storey Mountain*. It was published on March 2, 1949, just five months after *The Seven Storey Mountain*, and it rose to a high peak of popularity on the coattails of that best-seller (if I may mix metaphors a bit and speak of a book as having coattails). It went through a number of printings and by July had sold forty thousand copies, truly phenomenal for a book of its nature.

～～～～～～～～～～～ *The Title* ～～～～～～～～～～～

The title derives from a small booklet which Merton wrote in response to a letter from a student at St. Mary's College, Notre Dame. The student had asked: "What is Contemplation?" Merton responded with a manuscript and permission for St. Mary's to publish it. The manuscript's title was the same as the student's question: *What is Contemplation?* In it Merton wrote: "The seeds of this perfect life [that is, contemplative union with God] are planted in every Christian soul in Baptism. But seeds must grow before you reap the harvest.... *The seeds of contemplation* are planted...but (in so many cases) they merely lie dormant" (Templegate edition, p. 17).

The "seeds" metaphor has its roots, of course, in the Scripture. The parable of the seeds is in all three of the Synoptic Gospels. The parable is not just about seeds, it is also about the different kinds of soil that receive the seeds. That this parable was very much in Merton's mind is clear from the fact that he initially intended to call the book *The Soil and the Seeds of Contemplation*. If we recall that a parable is not a story that points a moral but rather one that is intended to challenge the hearer or reader, it can be rightly said that Merton's intent, like that of the parable of the seeds, is to confront his readers with the challenge: What kind of soil are you for the seeds of contemplation that God has sown in you?

~~~~~~~~~ **Inspiration for the Book** ~~~~~~~~~

If the title of the book came from a scriptural source, the inspiration for it came from Merton's confessor, Dom Gildas, who had told him, Merton said, "[t]o teach contemplation, and especially to let people know...that the contemplative life is quite easy and accessible and does not require extraordinary or strange efforts, just the normal generosity required to strive for sanctity" (*The Sign of Jonas*, p. 20, date of December 29, 1946).

Seeds was quite extensively reviewed, most of the reviews being favorable. The *Catholic Library World* called it a twentieth-century *Imitation of Christ*. The *London Literary Supplement*, however, put a finger on what may be the chief problem with the book: "There is so sharp a break and so deep a gulf between 'natural' and 'supernatural' that those who refuse the leap must be pardoned." A wise comment whose validity Merton would soon come to see.

Merton's own comments on the book were not happy ones. Though pleased with the burlap cover (which his publisher, James Laughlin, informed him was the kind of material being used for wall coverings in nightclubs), he voiced his misgivings with the book in an entry (March 6, 1949) in *The Sign of Jonas*: "Every book I write is a mirror of my own character and conscience. I always open the final, printed job, with a faint hope of finding myself agreeable, and I never do" (p. 165). He goes on: "There is nothing to be proud of in this one, either. It is clever and difficult to follow.... It lacks warmth and human affection. I find in myself an underlying pride that I had thought was all gone, but it is still there, as bad as ever. I don't see how the book will ever do any good." He laments that a book club that had taken it had hailed it as a streamlined *Imitation of Christ*. "God forgive me," he writes. "It is more like Swift than Thomas à Kempis."

Merton's dissatisfaction with the book moved him rather quickly to make at least some revisions in it. On July 9, 1949, he wrote to Jacques Maritain: "I am revising *Seeds of Contemplation*, in which many statements are hasty and do not express my true meaning." It is hard to disagree with Merton's disappointment with this book. It is a youthful book, often simplistic and naive, written by a young man who had turned his back on the world and seemed to want everybody to do the same.

He did produce a slightly revised edition that was published on December 19, 1949. The big revision, however, had to wait till 1961, when he produced *New Seeds of Contemplation*. *New Seeds* differs in many ways from its predecessors. "[It] is not," as Merton explains in the Preface, "merely a new edition of an old book." It is in many ways a completely new book. Minor changes have been made in the existing text and numerous additions to it. Most of the chapters have been expanded. A number of new chapters have been added. *Seeds* had twenty-seven chapters; *New Seeds*, thirty-nine. In my opinion, too much of the original has been retained. It would have been a better book if it had been totally rewritten. But Merton was always anxious to get on to something new: He did not have the patience that a thorough revision would have required. Still, *New Seeds* is a modern spiritual classic and one of the books for which Merton will be long remembered.

~~~~~~~~~~~ *Literary Genre* ~~~~~~~~~~~

It is a bit difficult to identify the literary genre to which *New*

Seeds (or *Seeds*) belongs. It has much to say about the contemplative experience, yet it is in no way a systematic study of that experience. Merton describes it as "a volume of more or less disconnected thoughts" (p. xiii); "a collection of notes and personal reflections" (p. xiv). It is like Pascal's work, a series of *pensées*, some developed more than others. Each chapter stands on its own and has no necessary connection with the chapter it follows or precedes, except that everything in the book is more or less about contemplative spirituality. Merton believes that many people, not just monks, have a hunger for the kind of things discussed in this book.

I have no intention of analyzing the contents of *New Seeds*. Suffice it to say that the dichotomy between the sacred and the secular (for which *Seeds* was criticized) has been overcome. "[R]eality is to be sought not in division but in unity, for we are 'members one of another'" (p. 47-48). "[I]n the depths of contemplative prayer there seems to be no division between subject and object, and there is no reason to make any statement either about God or about oneself. He IS and this reality absorbs everything else" (p. 267). "What happens [in contemplation] is that the separate entity that is *you* apparently disappears and nothing seems to be left but a pure freedom indistinguishable from infinite Freedom, love identified with Love. Not two loves, one waiting for the other, striving for the other, seeking for the other, but Love Loving in Freedom (283).... So it is with one who has vanished into God by pure contemplation. God alone is left. He is the 'I' who acts there. He is the one Who loves and knows and rejoices" (pp. 286-287).

I shall make no further comments. I refer you to the sections in Chapter Three of this book, which, you may remember, dealt with contemplative spirituality and the true self. Much of the material there is derived from this book. *New Seeds* belongs on the short list of the books one needs to read to understand Thomas Merton and his thought.

5. *Conjectures of a Guilty Bystander*

Conjectures is different in its literary genre from the four books we have discussed above, yet in some ways it includes elements of each of them. Thus, like *The Seven Storey Mountain*, it has bits of autobiography. Like *The Sign of Jonas*, there is journal material. (Merton explicitly states in the Preface: "The material is taken from notebooks I have kept since 1956.") The book was published in November 1966. So presumably it covers roughly ten years of his life-story—ten of what are certainly among the most significant years of that story.

Yet, unlike *The Sign of Jonas*, the items are not dated and do not seem to be in any exact chronological order. Nor are they simply taken verbatim from the journals. At times they include further reflections on journal items. To give but one example, the well-known experience of oneness with the whole human race that occurred at the corner of Fourth and Walnut Streets in Louisville (a key event in Merton's life that marked the beginning of his "return to the world") took place on March 18, 1958, yet it is not narrated till practically halfway through the book (pp. 156-158) and it is a considerable expansion of the narrative given for that date in the journal. (Compare Volume Three of the Merton journals, *A Search for Solitude*, pp. 181-182.)

Conjectures of a Guilty Bystander, made up as it is of items only loosely connected with one another, is somewhat like *No Man Is an Island* and *New Seeds of Contemplation*, yet the items tend to be much longer than the *pensées* of the earlier two. At the same time, whereas these earlier works were largely concerned with the interior life, *Conjectures* in large measure deals with issues of involvement in a world that has lost a sense of the contemplative. It's the "conjectures" of a Merton being pushed back into contact with the world by his contemplative experience.

The title Merton chose for this book gives some indication of where he was at this point in his life. What he offers his readers are not answers (as he had seemed all too

ready to do in some of his earlier books), but "conjectures."
By "conjectures" he means a probing of issues. The term
implies more than guesses, yet less than definitive positions.
Etymologically the word means "throwing [or putting] things
together" so as to arrive at a conclusion that appears
reasonable but by no means definitively so. In calling himself
a "bystander," Merton is referring to the aloofness of almost
two decades in the monastery, whereby he had distanced
himself from involvement in the problems of a world that, he
now realized, was after all his world, too. That distancing,
which he had at first considered the appropriate stance for a
monk, now implies for him a certain existential guilt. The
term "guilt" suggests two things: first, that for some time he
had failed to recognize the irresponsibility which that
aloofness involved, and second, that he should have
recognized it.

The Preface offers an important clarification of his
intentions for the book. It is, he tells us, his personal view of
the world in the 1960's. The book is not a soliloquy, but a
dialogue in which he seeks to talk with his readers and invite
their involvement in the questions. In no way is it a book of
prepackaged answers.

Though he speaks of various religious traditions, he is
careful to point out that it is not a book of professional
ecumenism, namely, the ecumenical endeavor to deal with
and attempt to resolve differences among religions. Such
interchange was important and necessary, but his interest lay
elsewhere: He wanted to seek those areas of religious
experience that united rather than divided people of various
religious backgrounds. His interest was in religious
experience rather then doctrinal formulations. In other
words, Merton feels obligated in the 1960's to do what the
Catholic Church was doing, namely, reaching out to the
contemporary world and to other religious traditions. He
invites his readers to join him on this venture. Thus he writes:

> If the Catholic Church is turning to the modern world and
> to other Christian Churches, and if she is perhaps for the
> first time seriously taking note of the non-Christian

religions in their own terms, then it becomes necessary for at least a few contemplative and monastic theologians to contribute something of their own to the discussion. This is one of the things this book attempts to do. It gives a monastic and personal view of these contemporary questions. The singular, existential, poetic approach is proper to this monastic view (p. 7).

Note the important statement "taking note of the non-Christian religions *in their own terms.*" Surely an approach was very new for the Catholic Church and something Merton embraced heartily.

Conjectures is a book for "dipping." I suspect that very few people read it through from beginning to end, nor is there any need to do so. While it is divided into five sections, the section titles are but a thin indication of content. I have found it helpful in teaching this book to suggest that it be seen as many pieces of a mosaic dealing with the great variety of issues that were on Merton's mind as he put this book together. The following is my own alphabetical arrangement of the pieces, with corresponding page numbers, which I recommend as a helpful approach for organizing one's reading of *Conjectures* (references are to the Image book edition):

1. **Autobiography:** 5-7, 89, 156-158, 180-189, 193, 200, 214, 245, 249, 257, 261-262, 280, 312, 320, 324.

2. **American Myth, the:** 33-39, 75-77, 80-81, 235-237.

3. **Death:** 41, 137-138, 189, 232-234, 262-263.

4. **Ecumenism:** 21, 33-39, 55, 76, 80, 101-102, 143-144, 168-171, 194-195, 203-205, 210-211, 217-218, 235-237, 270, 312-315, 323-326.

5. **Freedom:** 83, 88-90, 91-92, 115-116, 121, 166-171, 220-221, 227-229, 234, 237-238, 240, 250-251, 255.

6. **Latin American poets:** 13.

7. **Monasticism:** 150-151, 179-180, 184, 190-191, 199, 230-232, 244, 337-338.

6. *Zen and the Birds of Appetite*

Merton's contact with the great writers of the early Church and the Cistercian writers of the twelfth century established him clearly in a tradition that saw the contemplative experience as one that goes beyond verbalization, beyond rationalization. More and more he spoke of contemplation in terms of experience rather than in precise doctrinal statements. This emphasis on experience beyond concepts and words inevitably led him back to Eastern thought and especially to Zen. Before leaving for the East, Merton gathered together a number of his essays from different sources, all dealing with Zen, in a book he called *Zen and the Birds of Appetite*. I hesitated, for a while at least, about including this book among those I considered "must" reading to grasp something of the "essential" Merton. I hesitated because the book is difficult, challenging and demanding. Yet—and this was what moved me to include it—it is also splendid and insightful. One who takes the time to struggle with it will find it enormously rewarding. True, much of what is said here is expressed in other ways in books I have already recommended. But *Zen and the Birds of Appetite* shows, as no other work does, the clear grasp Merton had of Eastern thought: a way of life that was closer to his own Christian tradition than he had initially thought. It was, moreover, a means of enriching his understanding of that tradition.

It is a book that defies any effort to summarize. Its articles are quite varied, as the footnote at the beginning of each makes clear. Three were written for journals: "The Study of Zen," 1968, for the *Cimarron Review* of the University of Oklahoma; "New Consciousness," 1967, and "Transcendent Experience," 1966, for the *Newsletter* of the R. M. Bucke Society, Montreal. Two were prefaces to books: "A Christian Looks at Zen" (1966) was written as an introduction to a book by Merton's Chinese friend, Dr. John C. H. Wu, entitled *The Golden Age of Zen*; and "Nirvana," was a foreword to a dissertation by a Smith College student, Sally Donnelly. Two articles are tributes to well-known Zen masters: "D. T. Suzuki: The Man and his Works" and "Kitaro Nishida: A Zen Philosopher." There is one book review originally published in *The Catholic Worker*, August 1967, of *Zen in Japanese Art*, by Toshimitsu Hasumi (1962). Finally, the second part of *Zen and the Birds of Appetite* is made up of a lengthy dialogue (forty-nine pages) between Merton and Suzuki, called "Wisdom and Emptiness" and first published in *New Directions* magazine in 1961.

For a brief summary of the ideas basic to this book, see the section on Zen in Chapter Three, where I have discussed the "theme" of Zen.

7. The Asian Journal

In early 1968 Merton was invited to address an international Benedictine organization whose purpose was to help implement monastic renewal throughout the world. The organization was sponsoring a conference of all Asian monastic leaders, both Benedictine and Cistercian, to be held in Bangkok, Thailand, in December 1968. Merton was invited to give one of the principal addresses. With Abbot Flavian Burns's permission, he planned a trip that would take him to other countries besides Thailand. He flew out of San Francisco on October 15, 1968, with great joy in his heart and with "a great sense of destiny, of being at last on my true way after years of waiting and wondering and fooling around" (*The Asian Journal*, p. 4). The late Wilbur H. (Ping) Ferry, who had driven Merton about while he was in California, described him as he was about to board the plane: "Tom was as excited as a little kid on his first trip to Disneyland."

Thomas Merton went as a Christian monk deeply grounded by years of study in his own tradition and totally committed to it, yet, at the same time, deeply convinced that there was much he could learn from firsthand experience of Eastern monasticism. One of his early stops was in Calcutta, where he had been invited to address the Temple of Understanding meeting (a worldwide organization of religious leaders committed to communication among the religions of the world). In the notes he had prepared for this talk, which he gave on October 23, 1968, he had written:

> I think we have now reached a stage of (long-overdue) religious maturity at which it may be possible for someone to remain perfectly faithful to a Christian and Western monastic commitment, and yet to learn in depth from, say, a Buddhist or Hindu discipline and experience. I believe that some of us need to do this in order to improve the quality of our own monastic life and even to help in the task of monastic renewal which has been undertaken within the Western Church. (Ibid., p. 313)

Some might question the optimism with which Merton approached the East-West dialogue and the high hopes he had for its success. No one can question the enthusiasm with which he entered into the dialogue. In reading *The Asian Journal*, one is amazed at the untiring eagerness with which he recorded subtle and often esoteric Hindu and Buddhist texts in his notebook and the ease with which he seemed to establish instant rapport with the Dalai Lama and many other holy people whom he met on his journey.

But, though he was enthusiastic, he was not naive. He knew well the rules that must guide the dialogue. He spelled them out most clearly in the notes he prepared for the Calcutta talk: (1) The dialogue must be reserved for those who have been seriously disciplined by years of silence and a long habit of meditation. (2) It must avoid a false syncretism, by (3) scrupulously respecting important differences that exist between religious traditions. (4) It must not concentrate on secondary matters (such as institutional structure, monastic rules and suchlike), but on what is essential to the monastic quest, namely, the meaning and experience of self-transcendence and enlightenment achieved through transformation of consciousness. (See *The Asian Journal*, pp. 316-317.)

This kind of dialogue is crucial, he believed, for the monk has something important to say to contemporary men and women.

> It is the peculiar office of the monk in the modern world to keep alive the contemplative experience and to keep the way open for modern technological man to recover the integrity of his own inner depths. (Ibid., p. 317)

But, ultimately, communication through dialogue is not enough. Communication with words must yield place to communion without words: communion which, while it cannot dissolve differences, can in a certain way surmount them. Communion is sharing in a basic unity. Merton concluded his talk at Calcutta with these words:

> [T]he deepest level of communication is not communication, but communion.... It is beyond words...beyond concept. Not that we discover a new unity. We discover an older unity. My dear brothers [and sisters], we are already one. But we imagine that we are not. And what we have to recover is our original unity. What we have to be is what we are. (Ibid., p. 308)

In November Merton was in the Himalayas and on

November 4 had the first of three profoundly moving meetings with the Dalai Lama at Dharamsala. Merton found him impressive and likable. He was lively in conversation. His ideas of the interior life, Merton believed, were built on very solid ground and a real awareness of practical problems of life and the world. The Dalai Lama was also impressed by Merton. In his autobiography, published in 1990, the Dalai Lama said that the most striking thing about Merton was "the inner life he manifested. I could see he was a truly humble and deeply spiritual man. This was the first time that I had been struck by such a feeling of spirituality in anyone who professed Christianity.... [I]t was Merton who introduced me to the real meaning of the word 'Christian'" (*Freedom in Exile*, by Tenzin Gyatso [New York: HarperCollins, 1990], p. 189).

On December 2, there was the memorable trip to Polonnaruwa, an ancient ruined city in Sri Lanka, with its three gigantic Buddha figures carved out of stone. Victor Stier, attached to the United States embassy in Sri Lanka, who was Merton's host while he was there, wrote to "Ping" Ferry that Merton was tremendously impressed by the Polonnaruwa shrine. Merton's ecstatic reflections on the visit may be read in *The Asian Journal*:

> Looking at those figures I was suddenly, almost forcibly, jerked clean out of the habitual, half-tied vision of things, and an inner clearness...clarity, became evident and obvious.... [M]y Asian pilgrimage has come clear and purified itself. I mean, I know and have seen what I was obscurely looking for. I don't know what else remains but I have now seen and have pierced through the surface and have got beyond the shadow and the disguise. (pp. 235-36)

What was the surface he had pierced through? Was it that of Asia or of himself? The words seem to mean the first; they could also mean the second. Had Merton come halfway across the world to realize at last the experience of emptiness and that total transformation of consciousness that were the goal of his life? Had he, in the presence of the Buddha figures, at long last entered fully into the kenotic experience of the paschal mystery and put on the mind of Christ? We cannot answer these questions and perhaps we have no right to ask them. What we can do is reflect on the words he spoke on December 10 in the talk he had been invited to give to Christian monks and nuns at Bangkok.

> The monk is a man who has attained or is about to attain, or seeks to attain, full realization.... Not that he has acquired unusual or esoteric information, but he has come to experience the ground of his own being in such a way that he knows the secret of liberation and can somehow or other communicate this to others.... ✸

> The whole purpose of the monastic life is to teach men to live by love. The simple formula, which was so popular in the West, was the Augustinian formula of the translation of *cupiditas* into *caritas*, of self-centered love into an outgoing, other-centered love. In the process of this change the individual ego was seen to be illusory and dissolved itself, and in place of this self-centered ego came the Christian person, who was no longer just the individual but was Christ dwelling in each one. (*The Asian Journal*, pp. 333-334)

These are words he might have spoken to the monks at Gethsemani. It is indeed a paradox of divine Providence that this "pilgrim of the Absolute," who insisted that his monastery was not a "home," spoke these words thousands of miles away from his monastery; and then, in solitude, joined the company of "the burnt men" (*The Seven Storey Mountain*, p. 423; see also *The Sign of Jonas*, p. 224).

What Next? Letters, Journals, Other Works

If you have persevered up to this point and read all or some of the above books out of the Merton Library, you have probably fallen under the Merton spell and will go on reading him as much as you can. You will probably have an idea of which other books of his you wish to read. Hence I will simply conclude this chapter with a brief listing of other Merton books.

Between 1985 and 1994 the five volumes of the Merton letters were published. They must surely occupy a significant place in the Merton Library. As John Henry Newman once wrote: "The true life of a man is in his letters." Letters are a way of building and sustaining friendships. In the Merton letters you get to meet his many friends throughout the world. Letters give an insight into a person's humanness and concerns in ways that may not appear in books written for a general public. And, above all, Thomas Merton was a superb letter writer.

The titles of the five volumes of the letters will give some insight into the kind of letters you may expect to find in each volume:

Volume One. *The Hidden Ground of Love: Letters on Religious Experience and Social Concerns,* edited by William H. Shannon

Volume Two. *The Road to Joy: Letters to New and Old Friends,* edited by Robert E. Daggy

Volume Three. *The School of Charity: Letters on Religious Renewal and Spiritual Direction,* edited by Brother Patrick Hart

Volume Four. *The Courage for Truth: Letters to Writers,* edited by Christine M. Bochen

Volume Five. *Witness to Freedom: Letters in Times of Crisis,* edited by William H. Shannon

~~~~~~~~The Merton Journals~~~~~~~~~~

Merton had stipulated in his will that his journals were not to be published until twenty-five years after his death. Those twenty-five years have passed, so the journals are now in process of being edited. There will be seven such journals and their publication is expected to be completed by January 1998. The first five that have been published are:

Volume One. *Run to the Mountain: The Story of a Vocation: 1939-1941*, edited by Patrick Hart, O.C.S.O.

Volume Two. *Entering the Silence: Becoming a Monk and Writer: 1941-1952*, edited by Jonathan Montaldo

Volume Three. *A Search for Solitude: Pursuing the Monk's True Life: 1952-1960*, edited by Lawrence S. Cunningham

Volume Four. *Turning Toward the World: The Pivotal Years: 1960-1963*, edited by Victor A. Kramer

Volume Five. *Dancing in the Water of Life: Seeking Peace in the Hermitage: 1963-1965*, edited by Robert E. Daggy

Volume Six. *Learning to Love: Exploring Solitude and Freedom: 1966-1967*, edited by Christine M. Bochen (to be published in late 1997).

~.~Other Merton Books You Might Want to Read ~.~

Thoughts in Solitude (1959)

Disputed Questions (1960, see especially "Notes for a Philosophy of Solitude.")

Contemplation in a World of Action (1971)

Mystics and Zen Masters (1967)

The Literary Essays of Thomas Merton, edited by Brother Patrick Hart (1981)

The Way of Chuang Tzu (1965)

Day of A Stranger (1981)

The Collected Poems of Thomas Merton (1977)

Passion for Peace: The Social Essays of Thomas Merton, edited by William H. Shannon

In concluding this chapter, I shall just point out, without attempting to list or evaluate them, that there are many books, articles and dissertations about Merton. Some are better than others. But it goes beyond the intent of this chapter to classify or even to identify what has been written *about* Gethsemani's most famous monk.

Notes

[1] I am sure Merton would have intended to include in this last period, if he had remembered, *New Seeds of Contemplation* (1962) and *Cables to the Ace* (1968).

[2] Merton is not quite correct about his age. He would have been fourteen in 1929. That year he was in England and at Oakham School.

[3] On July 9, 1951, Robert Giroux wrote to tell Merton that *The Seven Storey Mountain* had gone into its 254th printing!

[4] Merton did try to write a book that contained much theological speculation. *The Ascent to Truth*, published in 1951, was an attempt to use the theological terminology of Saint Thomas Aquinas to explain the mystical experience of Saint John of the Cross. It was a work he agonized over more than any other. Though it contains some memorable passages, Merton, classifying his books some years later, listed *The Ascent to Truth* as only "FAIR." It is difficult to fault his classification.

Epilogue

In his book *The Silent Life* Merton says that a monk is a person whose whole life is devoted to the search for God. He is one for whom God alone suffices. Living a desert existence on the margins of society gives him a vantage point from which he can take up a critical attitude toward the world, its structures and the values it treasures. The reason he "leaves the world" is not to abandon it, but to free himself from its delusions so that he can offer it a vision of hope rooted in faith and love. But before he can offer that vision he must have experienced it in his own life. This is why contemplation is so crucial to his very existence and to his mission for the sake of the world. He cannot probe the heart of the world unless he has first sounded the depths of his own inner truth.

This is not to say that one becomes a contemplative *in order* to offer a message to the world. No, the contemplative life is justified by its own intrinsic meaning; it needs no purpose outside itself to validate it. But because he is a contemplative, the monk has (or should have) something of deep significance to say to the world.

To say that the contemplative has a vision to share and a message to proclaim is not to say that he or she has a blueprint which, if accepted, would solve the problems that beset today's world. The contemplative is not a problem-solver, but a prophet. He or she is the "troubler of Israel" who prods the consciences of people and directs their minds and hearts to the real issues of human existence. He or she is often "something of a rebel," but a faithful rebel—faithful to the divine word that is fire in their hearts. If they have achieved that purity of heart which is the fruit of contemplation, they are less likely to be taken in by the surface confusion that the world mistakes for reality. They are more likely to be committed to values that the world searches for, though not always knowingly: values that are permanent, deeply human and life-giving for the human spirit. Merton, for me, is one of the great prophets of our time and perhaps for generations to come.

On August 21, 1967, in response to a request from Pope Paul VI (sent through Dom Francois Decroix) for a message of contemplatives to the world, Merton wrote a moving letter to his sisters and brothers "in the world," which perhaps sums up the vision that he as a contemplative has to offer to them. He talks about the questions that "torment" people of our time:

> I do not know if I have found answers. When I first became a monk, yes, I was more sure of "answers." But as I grow old in the monastic life and advance further into solitude, I become aware that I have only begun to seek the questions. And what are the questions? Can man make sense out of his existence? Can man honestly give his life meaning merely by adopting a certain set of explanations which pretend to tell him why the world began and where it will end, why there is evil and what is necessary for a good life? My brother [and sister], perhaps in my solitude...I have been summoned to explore a desert area of man's heart in which explanations no longer suffice, and in which one learns that only experience counts.

He speaks of hope: "[I]t is my joy to tell you to hope.... Hope not because you think you can be good, but because God loves us irrespective of our merits and whatever is good in us comes from His love, not from our own doing." He concludes with a call to all of us:

> The message of hope the contemplative offers you, then, brother [and sister], is not that you need to find your way through the jungle of language and problems that today surround God: but that whether you understand or not, God loves you, is present to you, lives in you, dwells in

you, calls you, saves you, and offers you an understanding and light which are like nothing you ever found in books or heard in sermons. The contemplative has nothing to tell you except to reassure you and say that if you dare to penetrate your own silence and risk the sharing of that solitude with the lonely other who seeks God through you, then you will truly recover the light and the capacity to understand what is beyond words and beyond explanations because it is too close to be explained: it is the intimate union in the depths of your own heart, of God's Spirit and your own secret inmost self, so that you and He are in all truth One Spirit I love you, in Christ. (*The Hidden Ground of Love*, pp. 156-158)

Merton's Works Cited

Following is an alphabetical list of works by Thomas Merton, including collected letters, journals and essays, referred to in this book.

Ascent to Truth. New York: Harcourt, Brace, 1951.

Asian Journal, The. New York: New Directions, 1973.

Bread in the Wilderness. New York: New Directions, 1953.

Cables to the Ace. New York: New Directions, 1968.

Collected Poems of Thomas Merton, The. New York: New Directions, 1977.

Conjectures of a Guilty Bystander. Garden City, N.Y.: Doubleday, 1966.

Contemplation in a World of Action. Garden City, N.Y.: Doubleday, 1971.

Contemplative Prayer. Garden City, N.Y.: Doubleday, 1971.

Courage for Truth, The: The Letters of Thomas Merton to Writers, ed. Christine M. Bochen. New York: Farrar, Straus, Giroux, 1993.

Dancing in the Water of Life: Seeking Peace in the Hermitage, Journals of Thomas Merton, vol. 5, 1963-1965, ed. Robert E. Daggy. San Francisco: HarperSanFrancisco, 1997.

Day of a Stranger. Salt Lake City: Gibbs M. Smith, 1981.

Disputed Questions. New York: Farrar, Straus & Cudahy, 1960.

Emblems of a Season of Fury. New York: New Directions, 1963.

Entering the Silence: Becoming a Monk and Writer: Journals of Thomas Merton, vol. 2, 1941-1952, ed. Jonathan Montaldo. San Francisco: HarperSanFrancisco, 1996.

Exile Ends in Glory: The Life of a Trappistine, Mother M. Berchmans, O.C.S.O. Milwaukee: Bruce, 1948.

Faith and Violence: Christian Teaching and Christian Practice. Notre Dame, Ind.: University of Notre Dame Press, 1968.

Figures for an Apocalypse. Norfolk, Conn.: New Directions, 1948.

Gandhi on Non-Violence. New York: New Directions, 1965.

Hidden Ground of Love, The: The Letters of Thomas Merton on Religious Experience and Social Concerns, selected and edited by William H. Shannon. New York: Farrar, Straus, Giroux, 1985.

Honorable Reader: Reflections on My Work, ed. Robert E. Daggy. New York: Crossroad, 1989.

"Inner Experience, The." Unpublished.

"Labyrinth, The." Unpublished.

Last of the Fathers, The: Saint Bernard of Clairvaux and the Encyclical Letter, Doctor Mellifluus. New York: Harcourt Brace, 1954.

Life and Holiness. New York: Herder and Herder, 1963.

Literary Essays of Thomas Merton, The, ed. Brother Patrick Hart. New York: New Directions, 1981.

Living Bread, The. New York: Farrar, Straus & Cudahy, 1956.

Man in the Divided Sea, A. Norfolk, Conn.: New Directions, 1946.

Mystics and Zen Masters. New York: Farrar, Straus, Giroux, 1967.

New Man, The. New York: Farrar, Straus & Cudahy, 1961.

New Seeds of Contemplation. Norfolk, Conn.: New Directions, 1962.

No Man Is an Island. New York: Harcourt Brace, 1955.

Passion for Peace: The Social Essays of Thomas Merton, ed. William H. Shannon. New York: Crossroad, 1995.

Raids on the Unspeakable. New York: New Directions, 1966.

Road to Joy, The: Letters to New and Old Friends, ed. Robert E. Daggy. New York: Farrar, Straus, Giroux, 1989.

Run to the Mountain: The Story of a Vocation: Journals of Thomas Merton, vol. 1, 1939-1941, ed. Brother Patrick Hart, O.C.S.O. San Francisco: HarperSanFrancisco, 1995.

School of Charity, The: Letters on Religious Renewal and Spiritual Direction, ed. Brother Patrick Hart. New York: Farrar, Straus, Giroux, 1990.

Search for Solitude, A: Pursuing the Monk's True Life: Journals of Thomas Merton, vol. 3, 1952-1960, ed. Lawrence S. Cunningham. San Francisco: HarperSanFrancisco, 1996.

Seasons of Celebration. New York: Farrar, Straus, Giroux, 1965.

Seeds of Contemplation. New York: New Directions, 1949.

Seeds of Destruction. New York: Farrar, Straus, Giroux, 1964.

"Sentences." Mimeographed text.

Seven Storey Mountain, The. New York: Harcourt Brace, 1948.

Sign of Jonas, The. New York: Harcourt Brace, 1953.

Silent Life, The. New York: Farrar, Straus & Cudahy, 1957.

Spiritual Direction and Meditation. Collegeville, Minn.: Liturgical Press, 1960.

Strange Islands, The. New York: New Directions, 1957.

Tears of the Blind Lions. New York: New Directions, 1949.

Thirty Poems. 1944.

Thomas Merton: Spiritual Master: The Essential Writings, ed. Lawrence S. Cunningham. Mahwah, N.J.: Paulist Press, 1992.

Thoughts in Solitude. New York: Farrar, Straus & Cudahy, 1959.

Turning Toward the World: The Pivotal Years: Journals of Thomas Merton, vol. 4, 1960-1963, ed. Victor A. Kramer, San Francisco: HarperSanFrancisco, 1996.

Vow of Conversation, A: Journal, 1964-1965, ed. Naomi Burton Stone. New York: Farrar, Straus, Giroux, 1988.

Waters of Siloe. New York: Harcourt Brace, 1949.

Way of Chuang Tzu, The. New York: New Directions, 1965.

What Are These Wounds? Milwaukee: Bruce, 1950.

Wisdom of the Desert, The: Sayings From the Desert Fathers of the Fourth Century. New York: New Directions, 1960.

Witness to Freedom: Letters of Thomas Merton in Times of Crisis, ed. William H. Shannon. New York: Farrar, Straus, Giroux, 1994.

Zen and the Birds of Appetite. New York: New Directions, 1968.

Index

Merton Society), 11, 23, 48

J

Jenkins,
  Martha, 15
  Ruth, 7, 8
  Sam, 15
John Marie, Sr., 125
Johnston, William
  (*Christian Zen*), 118
Jones, Alan, 138

K

King, Rev. Dr. Martin
  Luther, Jr., 105, 114
Kirk, Grayson, 20

L

La Trappe, 27
Lax, Robert, 2, 20, 22
Leclercq, Jean, xi, 42
Lentfoehr, Therese, 151
Louis, Fr., see Merton, Thomas
Lycee Ingres, 9

M

Malits, Elena, 135
Marcus, Benjie, 2
Marcuse, Herbert, 104
Maritain, Jacques, 40, 158
Massignon, Louis, 42
Matthew, Brother, 27
Menchin, Robert, 28
Merton Annual, 48
Merton, John Paul, 8, 15
Merton, Owen, 7, 8, 10, 18
  artist, 8
  death of, 17
  in hospital, 12, 15
  in Algeria, 9
Merton, Ruth, 7, 8
Merton Seasonal, 11, 23, 48
Merton, Thomas,
  Alaska, 63
  American citizen, 3

as pilgrim, 137-138
birth, 1, 7
Catholic Church, reception
  into, 3, 4, 6
Clare College (Cambridge), 3, 19
Columbia University, 2, 5, 20
confirmation, 6
contemplation, 73
  and compassion, 37
  and solitude, 34
  and writing, 32-33
death, 43
eastern religions, early
  contact with, 61
ecumenism,
  his understanding
    of, 41-42, 161
experience of his father's
  presence, 18
freedom, stages of, 99-100
hermit, 35, 38
  and ecology, 39
  schedule, daily, 38
humanness, 49
images of, 58-67
journals, seven, 169-170
letter on contemplative
  life, 106, 174-175
letters, five volumes of, 169
Louisville, vision of, 35, 160
love for M., 40-41
master of novices, 35
Oakham, ix, 13, 16, 112
  debating team at, 13
rootedness, 66-67
solitude, desire for, 34
stability (of vocation), 29, 63-66
visit to Rome, 18
will of, 31
writings,
  articles:
    "Christian Culture Needs
      Oriental Wisdom," 50
    "Marxism and Monastic
      Perspectives," 43